The Rational Choice

Finding a Faith Rooted in Reality

*To Graham,
love Beccy*

Peter Tibbitts

Copyright © 2024 by Peter Tibbitts

All Rights Reserved

ISBN 13 – 9798344103341

No part of this publication may be reproduced, distributed or transmitted in any form or by any means, including photocopying, recording, or other electronic or mechanical methods, without the prior written permission of Peter Tibbitts, except in the case of brief quotations embodied in critical reviews and certain other non-commercial uses permitted by copyright law.

Dedication

This book is dedicated to my children;

Byron, Sarah, Amber, Sanjay, Samuel, Michael

and grandchildren; Oscar, Amber and bump(s),

and to my sisters; Tibi and Connie

My love for you prompted this writing,

so that 'you will know the truth

and the truth will set you free'.

It is further dedicated to my niece and nephews;

Jessica, Adam, Luke

and your spouses and children,

so that your faith may be strengthened.

And to my father, Jack, and my sister-in-law, Diana

who have been such a support to me in my journey.

And finally, to my deceased mother, Helen, and

brother, Steve,

who both loved me much, I miss you.

Table of Contents:

	Page
Introduction	7
Part 1: Why God	13
1. Universe	15
2. Our Solar System	20
3. Second Law of Thermo.	26
4. The Beginning of Life	29
5. Tackling Evolution	39
6. The Case Against Evolution	49
7. Other Thoughts	61
8. The Case For Evolution	79
9. The Conclusion of the Matter	82
Part 2: Why Christianity	85
1. Seeking the Truth	87
2. Beginnings and Historical Cont.	97
3. Purpose	108
4. Key People and Supernat. Events	111
5. The Historical Jesus	120
6. Saved by Grace	146
7. The Inner Witness	154
8. A Chronology of Our Relationship With God	159

Part 3: To Be a Christian	169
1. How to Become a Christian	173
2. The Principle of Grace	174
3. What Does 'Being a Christian' Mean?	177
4. Faith and Religion	186
5. The Spiritual Realm	191
6. Not a Bed of Roses	193
7. What About Baptism	196
Part 4: Which Christian Church	207
1. Beginnings and the Bible	209
2. The History of the Church	224
3. The Churches of Today	238
4. Beware the Wolves	246
5. Find a Church	257
Acknowledgments	259
About the Author	260

(Biblical quotes taken from the New International Version unless otherwise stated.)

The Rational Choice
*One faith **is** the **true faith.***

*The most important decision of your life is to find it, and make **the rational choice.***

Introduction:

Rooted in reality? Sometimes you find yourself in one of these conversations where one person after another is stating, "well I believe that…" in response to some big philosophical question like, "What is the meaning of life?" or "What happens after we die?" or "What spirituality governs our existence?". Some think that the answers to those questions can be whatever you want them to be - 'your' reality. The confusion arises from experience. Two people may have an interaction, which could be recorded on video. Each person has their own unique experience of the interaction, 'their' reality, but it cannot alter what is on the video, what I would call the objective reality. In this context, their experienced realities are usually more important or significant to their lives, it impacts their feelings, their relationships, and their future behaviour, it may even cause their recall of the interaction to differ from what is on the video. Hence, each experienced reality is more valid to that person, and it becomes their truth. But, their experienced reality, their 'truth', cannot alter the objective reality of what is on the video, nor can one's experienced reality alter the true, objective answers to most of the big philosophical questions.

In the case of religion or beliefs, many people use their experience to determine their beliefs, whether that is praying to the sun and having a good harvest leading to a system of sun worship; or the more familiar, "I can't believe in a God who would let ..... happen". Rather than starting from an objective reality and using that to interpret and try to understand our experience, we use our experience to formulate a belief from which to interpret our future experience. It becomes a self-fulfilling prophecy, to a degree, and we can become trapped within our own experience-based belief system.

To go back to the interaction between the two people, what if one person's experienced reality was mistaken? What if they mis-interpreted, or misunderstood the other person's intention or body language or words? Now they have a 'truth' that mis-shapes their attitude and behaviour towards the other person, and wrongly guides their future interpretation of interactions with this other person to reinforce their 'truth'. And potentially, they become entrenched in a misguided 'truth'. How common this is in our daily lives and relationships, and how natural it is to extend this system of "belief based on experienced reality" well beyond relationships.

The Rational Choice

So how do we not go down this path of beliefs based on experienced reality? Well, in everyday life, this is moderated by "keeping an open mind". This means keeping attitudes and beliefs plastic (flexible) so that they can be continually revised and modified as new experiences provide new, and sometimes conflicting, data. But with the bigger issues, that are not part of everyday life and yet inform our core attitudes, a bit more intentionality is needed, and this is where the Scientific method proves useful. This method involves collecting objective data and then formulating models and beliefs that are consistent with that data. Then, additional objective data is used to refine the model, or belief, and make predictions from the model to be tested and further confirm or refine the model.

For me, and I think most people, the answers to the big philosophical questions must lie in a reality that is objective, outside of me and my experienced reality, and rooted in a reality that is consistent with the objective data of life, our world, and the universe we live in. In other words, it is not what one believes that shapes reality, but rather it is reality that should shape what one believes.

Whether there is one God (Judeo-Christian), a multitude of gods (Hindu) or no gods at all (Buddhist) does not depend upon one's belief. We can live as if our belief is true, we can act as if our belief is true, and we can interpret the world and events as if our belief is true, but that doesn't make our belief true; rather it limits our lives to a framework or bondage that comes with our belief. And then comes the reckoning, when we die and are confronted with true reality, and we can no longer define reality as we choose – it is out of our hands.

This is what forms the initial purpose of this book, to present the evidence, the 'data', demonstrating that life, our world, and the universe all point to the objective reality of God, and Jesus Christ as God incarnate; that the Christian Faith is the rational choice.

The second purpose of this book is to consider, briefly, what it means to our lives today, and in the future, for the Christian faith to be reality, to understand the distinction between Christian faith and Christian religion, and to consider how to navigate our way in the Christian religion, in order to grow in Christian faith. This last phrase may sound a bit odd, but much distracting, misleading and even false religiosity can be found in the Christian religion. Just as Jesus' fiercest opponents were the religious leaders, and traditional doctrines, of the Jews, so much of today's fiercest opposition to the Christian faith is entrenched denominationalism and the religious leaders within those denominations, along with their doctrines and traditions. In Part 3 of the book, I will delineate the basic principles of the Christian faith and use them, in Part 4, as a lens to view the challenging and complex Christian expression of today.

The goal of this book is to help people to see Christianity not as a religion to choose, but as a reality to embrace, and then to help them to grow in this reality rather than be overcome by the religiosity that necessarily springs up in all Christian organisations (like the wheat and the tares – the fake is always sown among the true). Ultimately my goal is to grow, and help others grow, in the knowledge and love of God our Father, Jesus our Saviour, and Holy Spirit our counsellor.

12

The Rational Choice

Part 1: Why God

14

The Rational Choice

Chapter 1 Universe

As far as we know, everything that exists, physically, is contained in our universe, the only universe. There are theories of multiple universes, but those theories have significant problems, and for all intents and purposes are more intellectual debate than pragmatic reality. Within our universe are **billions** of galaxies (yes, billions!!!), each containing **billions** of stars, and just one of these galaxies is our galaxy, the Milky Way, in which resides one particular star, our star, the Sun. You'll notice that in this cosmic description of the universe, planets, moons, asteroids, comets and all the other stuff isn't even mentioned. All these things are just seemingly insignificant specks of matter orbiting around the main players, the stars.

Now let's turn this around and view it in the other direction. We are living on this incredible planet, Earth, as it spins around like a top while silently following this endless circular path around a ball of superheated plasma and gases which we call our Sun. Our Sun is a star, medium to small in size, as stars go. The Sun is the centre of our solar system, keeping all of its host of bodies (planets, asteroids, comets, etc.) in orbits around it by a tremendous gravitational force field produced by its huge mass. (Over 99% of the total mass of our solar system is in the Sun.) The Sun looks really big, to us, as it is fairly close to our Earth, just 8 light minutes away, or 150 million kilometres (a distance that would take 3 to 4 months for a very fast rocket). The next closest star to us is Proxima Centauri, at a distance of 4.2 light years away (about 270,000 times greater than the Sun-to-Earth distance), and that looks like a typical twinkling speck of light in the night sky. The Sun and Proxima Centauri are just two of the billions of stars orbiting a black hole, that make up our Milky Way galaxy. That makes the size of our galaxy beyond my spatial comprehension. And then, millions of light years beyond our galaxy is another galaxy, with billions of stars, named Andromeda galaxy, followed by over a **billion more galaxies** separated by millions and billions of light years. This, then, is our universe, huge beyond comprehension.

However, our universe is finite. It does not go on forever, although it may seem to. Our universe has a size, and in 1927, it was proposed by a Belgian Catholic Priest / physicist, Georges Lemaitre, that it is getting bigger; that the universe is expanding. He came to this conclusion by working on some equations that Einstein had come up with having to do with his theory of relativity. Einstein concurred with Lemaitre's mathematics but was not happy with the physics it proposed – this expanding universe. Within a couple years, Edwin Hubble published his work confirming the expanding universe idea with a

The Rational Choice

decade of observed evidence of galactic red shifts (light colour changes from distant galaxies indicating their relative movement to us). By 1931, Lemaitre was extending this expanding universe theory to the idea of it having expanded out from a single point, a "primordial atom" which he referred to as "the Cosmic Egg exploding, at the moment of creation".

Almost two decades later, in 1948, other physicists predicted that if Lemaitre was right with this primordial atom idea, along with subsequent refinements of this theory, there should be a common microwave radiation observed on Earth, coming from every direction in the universe which has subsequently come to be known as Cosmic Microwave Background Radiation. This theory of an expanding universe with a beginning, the Big Bang Theory (so named by Fred Hoyle in a sarcastic remark reportedly made in 1949 while arguing against the theory), was in conflict with the previously held Steady State Theory (suggesting the universe has always been – hence no beginning). It wasn't until the 1960s that the accidental discovery of Cosmic Microwave Background Radiation by Penzias and Wilson confirmed the 1948 predictions and ended the debate. The Big Bang Theory of the origin of the universe is now overwhelmingly accepted as the scientific explanation of our universe's beginning, being supported by over a century of astronomical and cosmological evidence.

However, this previous debate between the Steady State Theory and the Big Bang Theory was further complicated by a conflict of beliefs. The Big Bang Theory was proposed by a Catholic Priest, one whose belief system held to the idea that the universe was created, hence it had a beginning. The Steady State Theory held to a universe that has always been, hence no beginning, no initial cause, and thus had the support of atheists. So, the Big Bang Theory was seen as coming out of a Christian belief system. How ironic that it is now so commonly, mistakenly, seen as being in conflict with Christian beliefs. In fact, the objective evidence supports the idea that the universe had a beginning, which is consistent with the Christian faith, along with most monotheistic faiths, but causes problems for atheistic beliefs because there had to be a cause behind the beginning of the universe. If it had a beginning, there had to be something that caused it to begin, and this is where atheistic views get stuck. What caused the universe to begin?

To extend this discussion just a little further, there is the idea of sequential universes, which may seem an attractive proposal, but evidence found in the last 20 years or so has all but eliminated any potential credence it may have had. This idea held that a universe would start with a big bang and then expand to a limit where gravity would eventually win and pull the universe back together into a big crunch, commencing the big bang of the next universe, much like a ball thrown up in the air and eventually reaching a peak before being pulled back down only to bounce on the ground and start over again. This allowed for a seemingly unbroken succession of universes for eternity, and hence no beginning. However, for the last 20 years or so, there has been overwhelming evidence to suggest that our universe expansion is speeding up (as if the ball thrown upwards speeds up and flies off into outer space rather than falling back down) and thus there will be no big crunch. This effect is tied up with dark energy, of which a small part is dark matter, which is thought to provide the force causing the accelerating expansion. Hence, there is no big crunch, there is no evidence to support successive universes, and we are again faced with the objective evidence indicating that the universe had a beginning and thus a cause.

Chapter 2 Our Solar System

So, the universe began, and it seems that the general consensus points towards it happening about 14 billion years ago, based on a very large amount of astronomical observations, measurements and calculations (most, if not all of which involve the speed of light). It is also generally agreed that out of the Big Bang came energy and all sorts of massive, unstable particles which decayed to form the elements Hydrogen and Helium, and no others. These gases eventually clumped up into massive gas clouds, nebulae, where further coalescing led to the formation of the first generation of stars. The lighter elements of the Periodic Table (the table of the elemental building blocks of matter throughout the universe) were formed through nuclear fusion in the cores of these stars. These stars proceeded through their 'life cycle' until they exploded in supernova events producing the remaining elements of the Periodic Table, and distributing these elements, as gases and dust, throughout the universe. From these supernovae came the ingredients for the formation of our solar system (and all solar systems for that matter).

Now, regarding time, the 14 billion years age of our universe makes sense from two perspectives. First, the astronomical measurements, including galactic recession speeds (how fast galaxies are moving apart), provide data which leads to the calculation of 14 billion years. But secondly, the time needed for a generation of stars to proceed through a 'life cycle' and supernova, producing the interstellar medium necessary for the formation of our Solar System, which is subsequently dated at 4½ billion years, leads to an estimate of the age of the universe of over 10 billion years. This age evidence, from the two perspectives, strongly conflicts with any 'recent creationist' views of the universe having an age of less than 100,000 years. *(see footnote below)*

(footnote: the Genesis account of creation has two major interpretations of the 7 days; first that they were short periods of time or literal days meaning it happened in the recent past (less than 100,000 years) or second that they represented eras, or very large time periods meaning it occurred in ancient times (billions of years ago). Believers of the former are referred to as 'recent creationists' and believers of the latter are referred to as 'ancient creationists'.)

Interestingly, the various parts of our solar system seemed to form at roughly the same time, hence the sun, earth and moon are all about the same age. And the water of our solar system predates the massive bodies as it was formed in the nebula cloud. So the Earth and moon could have formed as bodies prior to the sun beginning to radiate visible light.

At this point, the scientific evidence points towards the following:

- The universe had a beginning
- It began with a burst of seemingly infinite energy
- It expanded, and cooled, and emitted electromagnetic radiation, including visible light, and what later would be discovered as cosmic microwave background radiation
- Protons and electrons formed, giving rise to the element Hydrogen, and through early fusion, the element Helium
- A first generation of stars formed and died, in supernovae, producing the interstellar medium necessary for the formation of subsequent solar systems
- From a nebula cloud of gas and dust our solar system formed with the sun, earth and moon all being formed about 4½ billion years ago
- The Earth and moon may have formed prior to the Sun becoming a light emitting star (main sequence)
- Water was present in the nebula cloud prior to the forming of the Sun, Earth and moon

First and foremost, the beginning of the universe, the Big Bang, has no plausible explanation apart from being caused by something pre-existing and greater, ie the ultimate 'designer', God. Then we are faced with the fact that no human, prior to our modern age, could have the above understanding of the origins of our planet, sun, solar system, etc. apart from being informed of such by God, or spiritual beings pre-existing the universe. With this in mind, imagine that God communicated the creation process to mankind, over 5000 years ago. Imagine what that would sound like, how that could be expressed to a pre-modern era person, and compare this with the Genesis account below:

> In the beginning, God created[1] the heavens and the earth. Now the earth was formless[2] and empty, darkness[3] was over the surface of the deep, and the Spirit of God was hovering over the waters.
>
> God said, "Let there be light[4]." – first day
>
> God said, "Let there be an expanse between the waters to separate water from water[5], and He called the expanse 'sky'". – second day
>
> God said, "Let the water under the sky be gathered together (seas)[6] and let dry ground appear (land). Let the land produce vegetation[7], seed bearing." – third day

Why God

God said, "Let there be lights in the sky, to give light on the earth." God made two great lights, the greater to govern the day and the lesser to govern the night[8]. He also made the stars[9]. – fourth day

Taking this account from Genesis, the first book of the Bible, consider this breakdown of its sequence of statements (numbered in the text) through the lens of modern understanding:

1. First it has a beginning, and it was created by a pre-existing God.
2. Earth was in the process of forming from coalescing gas and dust.
3. The sun was not yet producing light.
4. This light, first day, is back at the start, the Big Bang. God spoke, with a seemingly infinite energy to start creation, and as the universe expanded and cooled, light was emitted, from everywhere, ending the darkness (the absence of light). Note that this was not the light of the sun, or contemporary stars for that matter, but it could have included light from the first generation of stars.
5. The waters in the nebula cloud were divided into those for the earth and those for the rest of the solar system. Additionally, the early upper atmosphere may have been loaded with water

vapour like a global cloud to protect the earth from the harmful radiation to come from the sun.
6. The waters on the earth formed seas around a land mass (the Pangaea?).
7. The vegetation here, day 3, may be spoken of as that which is to be produced from the land but not yet in form. (perhaps the seeds of vegetation)
8. The sun finally starts to shine (fusion begins and it enters its main sequence phase) and hence the moon starts to reflect the sun's light. Hence, sun, earth and moon all forming at roughly the same time.

For a creation narrative over 5000 years old, this has an amazing likeness to our scientific understanding of today. It is worth noting that such a creation narrative is unique to the Judeo-Christian belief, and those belief systems derived from it, which will be discussed in Part 2.

Chapter 3 Second Law of Thermodynamics

Thermodynamics is pretty complex stuff with far reaching consequences, but of course it reduces down to some seemingly simple, basic rules called the Laws of Thermodynamics, of which there are 4.

1. Zeroth law: If two systems are each in thermal equilibrium with a third system, then they must be in thermal equilibrium with each other.
2. First law: Energy is conserved, it cannot be created or destroyed but rather it can only change form. (Note that matter is also a form of energy.)
3. Second law: The entropy of an isolated system can only increase with time. It cannot decrease. (The arrow of time, disorder must increase)
4. Third law: The entropy of a system approaching absolute zero temperature approaches a constant minimum value.

The last two of these laws are about a concept called entropy which can be described in several different ways, but it is usually referred to as the disorder or randomness of a system. It can also be described as the lack of availability of a system's thermal energy for doing mechanical work.

Basically, this Second law states that disorder must increase, and that the universe is running down like a wound-up clock. This is shocking! This is a law of Physics, not a theory or idea or a maybe, but an uncompromising, unchanging, unbreakable law. This is a fact.

So, let's consider a straightforward example of how this law applies.

> I start with a random pile of bricks and I stack them up. It appears that I have made order from disorder. However, quite the opposite has happened. I have used my thoughts/plans to create an ordered system of bricks, but it required me to expend energy through my muscles to stack those bricks into an ordered system, and my muscles took an ordered system of chemicals (my body's stored energy) and converted them to a less ordered system while producing heat which was lost to the air around me, warming my surroundings and producing more disorder. Altogether, the increase in disorder exceeded the small increase in order of the bricks and entropy won.

From this we see that although entropy always wins, increases in order can take place where energy and information are supplied from outside as long as the total change in entropy (randomness), overall, is positive. We see this in all aspects of our lives and experience. We grow, we make things, we order things, but always by supplying energy and information so that overall, entropy increases. We also see that everything we make, ordered systems, deteriorates over time into disordered systems.

So, what does this have to do with our universe? Clearly, our universe had to start like a wound-up clock of minimum entropy and maximum potential for useful work. It had to start in a highly ordered state with an incredible system of laws and physical constants, rules governing how the physical universe behaves, how atoms are structured and how molecules and ionic structures must form. Most of us think of the Big Bang as a cosmic explosion of extraordinary disorder, when in fact it was an event of mind-boggling order, not to mention, an event of creation.

The Big Bang didn't break the laws of thermodynamics, it started them. It was an event outside of time in the sense that it was the beginning of time. It provided the sum-total of energy from which the first law goes on to describe its conservation. It provided the infinite order from which the second law proceeds to erode away. What could have caused the Big Bang short of something of infinite energy, infinite order, infinite information and outside of time. Sounds like God.

Chapter 4 The Beginning of Life

So far, in discussing the universe, our solar system and the Big Bang, we have been looking at the physical universe, but not life. Here we will look at the beginning of life on Earth, and what we mean by life.

In secondary schools around the British Isles, and I suspect the world, the Science curriculum has been describing living things as having 7 characteristics (Mrs Gren is an acronym known by many, at least here in Britain); they are:

Movement, Respiration, Sensitivity, Growth, Reproduction, Excretion, and Nutrition.

This description includes plants as living things, having the capacity for movement and sensitivity (root growth towards water, leaves turning toward the sun, etc.), using oxygen for energy at a cellular level, growing and reproducing, taking in nutrients and eliminating waste products (CO_2). Rocks could potentially grow (eg. sedimentation), but that is the extent of it. And it is generally taught that in order to meet these 7 characteristics, the living thing must be a cell or have a cellular structure. Hence many would say that a virus is not in fact a living thing although it is made of organic material.

Then there is the concept of thought. Hence, I would go even further to suggest that plants are a rudimentary form of life, but that a fuller sense of life requires the capacity for thought, in other words, a brain. Thus, I am recognising a distinction between the plant kingdom and the animal kingdom with regards to the degree of life, which I will come back to in the next chapter.

So, the next question is how did the existence of life (plant or animal) come into being, or what some refer to as biogenesis? This is not yet anything to do with evolution, but rather how it started in the first place. How did cells form without pre-existing cells? One look in an advanced level Biology textbook gives a brief glimpse into the incredible complexity of a cell, and the multiple structures required for a functional cell. Where did the building blocks come from and how were they organised into the structures and overall configuration necessary?

From the Big Bang we got the elements Hydrogen and Helium. Later, from stars and their supernova events the universe was filled with the dust of the remaining elements we list today in the periodic table. Everything tangible is made from combinations of atoms and ions of these elements. These are the building blocks of the physical universe, but the building blocks of living systems are amino acids. Amino acids are specific combinations of atoms of carbon, nitrogen, oxygen and hydrogen which are the bricks used to make proteins, from which the structures of a cell are made. Amino acids are not the only building blocks of living organisms (others include lipids, carbohydrates and nucleic acids), but they are essential. For humans, there are 20 different amino acids needed for the proteins of our bodies, 11 of which can be formed by our bodies (because we have pre-programmed synthesizing mechanisms in our cells) and 9 of which cannot be formed, and we must consume them in our diets (called essential amino acids).

So where did these amino acids come from and where did the synthesizing mechanisms come from, both for the 11 made in our bodies and for the 9 made outside our bodies? Over 60 years ago, an experiment was carried out called the Miller-Urey experiment, where sparks, produced in a mixture of water vapour, ammonia, methane and hydrogen, caused some amino acids to be formed. Further experiments over the last 60 years have confirmed that natural synthesis of amino acids could have been possible in Earth's early atmosphere through lightning, solar radiation or some possible means of catalysis. But consider, how was it possible to form the biological systems necessary for replicating these amino acids and for making the RNA and DNA necessary for sequencing them into specific proteins, and then configuring these proteins into unique structures and tissues to form the parts of a cell or an organism? Also problematic is the fact that nearly all the amino acids are chiral, meaning they can be "right handed" or "left handed" in their structure, and for protein synthesis, they must be the correct "handedness", not a mixture of both. Yet, in their non-biological synthesis, a mixture of both would be formed rather than the necessary single "handedness".

Hence, we are faced with the following dilemma regarding the origin of life: There are **plausible** theories (not necessarily probable) of how **some** of the necessary chemical building blocks of life, such as amino acids, could have first formed through natural processes in an early Earth atmosphere, however the theories and plausibility rapidly diminish with further inspection such as:

- How could these amino acids be sequenced into useful proteins non-biologically
- How could biological systems of amino acid synthesis have developed
- How could any proteins be organised into useful and co-functional structures (eg. forming a cell wall or membrane)
- How could useful forms of RNA and DNA have formed?

These are words, easily read, and easy to gloss over, so we need to see a picture. The most fundamental unit of all living organisms is a single cell. Hence the beginning of living organisms is the beginning of cells. But a cell is anything but a simple structure that could form by random chance. On the next two pages are simple diagrams of the two basic types of cells, plant and animal, which could be found in most Biology textbooks:

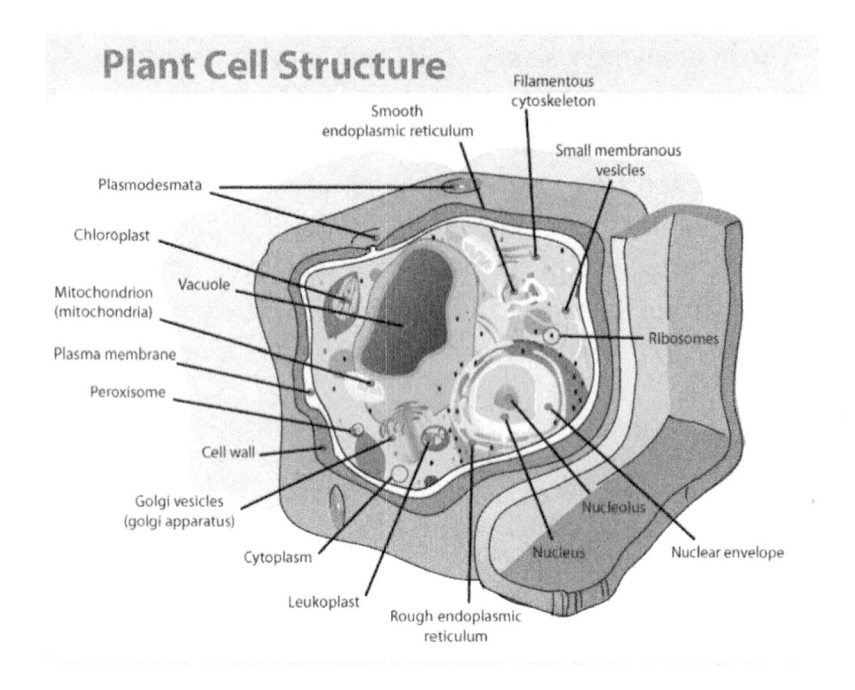

Attribution: LadyofHats, CC BY-SA 4.0, via Wikimedia Commons

The Rational Choice

Animal cell structure

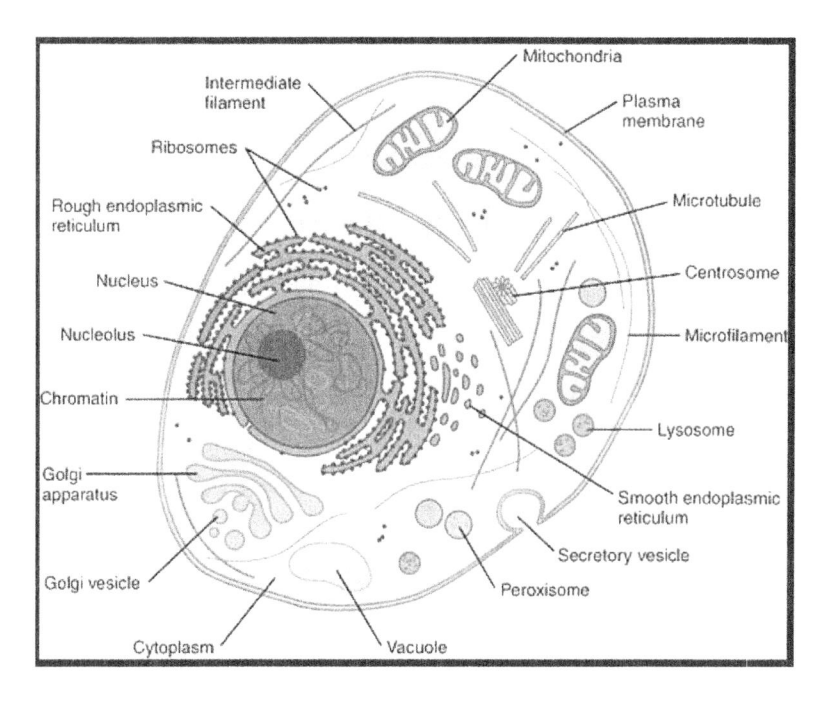

Attribution: OpenStax, CC BY 4.0, via Wikimedia Commons

You can see from either of these diagrams the incredible complexity of a 'simple' cell. They are microscopic factories, and what is more, each organelle or component of a cell is itself a very complex structure. Even the

Why God

membrane surrounding each cell is a highly complex structure.

Cell Membrane

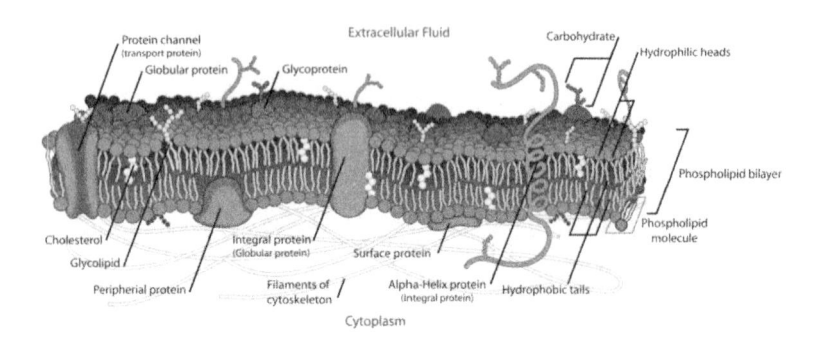

Attribution: LadyofHats, CC BY 4.0, via Wikimedia Commons

This is complicated! Cells are complicated; yet these are the basic units of life, so how did they come about? A basic cell, with all its necessary, and interdependent organelles, having very complex structures in their own rights, how did it come about? There is no conceivable evolutionary process by which this could happen. There is no stepwise process to evolve a cell. In a sense, the theory of evolution begins with a fully functional, reproducing cell, so even that can't be called upon. The

Miller-Urey experiment suggesting a possible origin of amino acids doesn't touch it. Any outer space suggestion (from extra-terrestrial origins) also just pushes the question back in time but still leaves the question. There certainly is no scientific answer, apart from the scientific method of examining the data and proposing a plausible theory to explain that data, with the only plausible theory being a creative act of God, which cannot be tested scientifically. (As Sherlock Holmes stated, "When you have eliminated the impossible, whatever remains, however improbable, must be the truth.")

So, why is there no mention of God in our schools' Biology textbooks? With no plausible scientific theory to explain the origins of a cell, of life, why is the only alternative, God, ignored? Is it because we have started from a biased position of excluding the possibility of God? Or have we diverted our attention away from a **seemingly** unanswerable question (does God exist) to others that we can address, and thereby avoided the inevitable conclusion that He must exist? Or, finally, have we never actually felt confronted with the question in the first place, until now? You can't have a clock without a clockmaker, and you can't have a cell without God.

Why God

In fact, I think God is excluded from our Biology textbooks (all Science textbooks for that matter) because God created Science, so God has to be outside of the rules and constraints of Science. Unfortunately, this leads to the bias of excluding God from our mindset, or assuming there is no God, simply because the explanation exceeds that of which Science can address. Hence the textbooks start with the cells and don't address how they came to exist in the first place. Similarly, the Theory of Evolution, which I will address in the next chapter, starts with the cells and moves on from there, ignoring how the cells themselves came into existence.

Chapter 5 Tackling Evolution

The Theory of Evolution is very attractive owing to its relative simplicity and its apparent agreement with our common experience. We understand that mutations happen, we observe the Survival of the Fittest process, and we imagine that anything could happen given a long enough time period (millions of years). We see how diverse people groups have developed from a common ancestral group through geographical isolation, and we see the results of selective breeding in dogs, cats and cattle. It starts with a simple beginning, and then through infinitesimal changes (or maybe not so infinitesimal step changes) occurring through millions of generations, across millions, or billions of years of time, a plethora of incredibly complex, multi-organed creatures (including us) have developed. Yet, as I read what I have written, I am stunned by the incredible magnitude, and even improbability or impossibility of what it suggests. We are lulled into accepting it because 'it is scientific' and it allows an explanation other than 'God did it', and because the 'survival of the fittest' element of it seems to work. If we just focus on gibbons evolving into humans it begins to look plausible (so many similar features), but we ignore the amoeba to gibbon transition by accepting that anything is possible given enough time. In fact, we accept it because we don't, maybe can't, look more deeply into it and seriously question its plausibility. 'Scientists far smarter than myself accept it so who am I to question it?' However, if we do question it, we'll find that the theory of evolution crumbles relatively easily as a 'scientific theory' and the greater marvel is why it is still accepted and taught at all.

To begin with, the theory of evolution has two main parts: constructive mutations and natural selection. It holds that mutations can occur in reproduction which afford the next generation an advantage towards procreation and / or survival, and then through natural selection the mutated form prospers and out-survives the unmutated form, leading to an enhanced organism. The theory then extrapolates this further to even crossing genetic boundaries between different types of organisms. So, we must look at these two parts, constructive mutations and natural selection, separately, and in the light of the genetic knowledge that has been gained since Darwin's proposal back in 1859.

Constructive Mutations:

This part needs to be broken down further into two sub-sections; constructive mutations within a specie and constructive mutations across species or genetic boundaries. The first of these, within a specie, still begins with 'constructive mutations'. It is essential to understand that mutations are errors in replication and not just variants within the range of normal replication. In the two forms of cellular reproduction, mitosis and meiosis, the genetic information of chromosomes is copied, either wholly as in mitosis or as a variant as in meiosis.

To use human cells as an example, each cell contains 23 pairs of chromosomes, or a total of 46 chromosomes, and these will be an individual's genetic blueprint. A **chromosome** is a long DNA chain of many segments in which the segments are **genes** that determine or influence one or more aspects of our physical makeup such as hair colour or nose shape. Within a pair of chromosomes, each chromosome has the same basic function or gene sequence, but the genes are not identical so a gene on one chromosome may suggest blue eyes while that on the other chromosome may suggest brown eyes, and the individual would have brown eyes as that is the dominant gene.

In mitosis, all 46 chromosomes are copied identically and the new set of 46 chromosomes separates from the original set leading to a new, essentially identical cell forming. This is how growth and repair takes place in our bodies. Mutations, or errors in this replication, lead to faulty cells or even cancerous cells.

In meiosis, a random selection of genes from each pair of chromosomes in the parent is copied to produce a single set of 23 chromosomes, called a gamete. When this gamete from a male (sperm) fuses with a gamete from a female (egg), fertilisation takes place and a new cell of 23 pairs (46 chromosomes) is formed. This cell will replicate by mitosis to form a ball of cells leading to an embryo. In the meiosis, and subsequent mitosis into a ball of cells (and even into differentiation), any fault in replication will result in a mutation as these cells are the blueprint for all subsequent cells to be made (stem cells).

This (meiosis) is where the opportunity for variation within a specie will occur and thus selective breeding or natural selection. The variation results from the random selection of genes in meiosis, and the selective breeding involves directing this 'random' selection by choosing who to mate with who (and who not to mate), thereby giving certain genes a higher probability of selection.

Meiosis is also where mutations can occur resulting in altered offspring, a key element of evolution. A mutation would occur when an error in the replication process forms a defective gamete and this becomes part of the genetic makeup of a new organism, or when the gamete itself is damaged (say by radiation causing molecular damage to the DNA chain in the mother's egg cell or father's sperm cell) and that gamete goes on to become part of the genetic makeup of a new organism. Thus, the new organism, still the same type of organism, will have a defective genetic code that may or may not express itself.

Hence, mutations can result from a mistake in the replication process resulting in a permanent fault in the genetic code of the offspring, or from acquired damage in the genetic code of the parent's reproductive cells, or from acquired damage or replication errors in the stem cells early in embryonic development which is replicated into the genetic code of the offspring. Whichever way, replication error or acquired damage, the new genetic code of the offspring is not just different, it is defective. The theory of Evolution requires that this defective code may sometimes be advantageous to the offspring's survival and potential to procreate, and therefore may result in a genetic code that prospers and becomes dominant in the population as a result of Natural Selection. That 'beneficial' defective code is a big flaw in the theory, but that is not all.

In addition to these random deviations in the genetic code, there needs to be changes in the number of chromosomes in order to evolve into different types of organisms. And the number of chromosomes in an organism is not an indication of its complexity or cognitive ability. For example, here is a small list of animals and plants with their respective number of chromosomes:

Fruitfly	8
Pea	14
Kangaroo	16
Tiger, Cat, Sea Otter	38
Mango, Beaver, Peanut	40
Human, Muntjac deer	46
Gorilla, Orangutan, Chimpanzee	48
Strawberry	56
Horse	64
White-tailed Deer	70
Dog	78
Turkey	80
Carp	100
Rattlesnake	184
Red King Crab	208
Black Mulberry	308
Shrimp	508

Somehow, for evolution to have occurred, these mutations would have also included the addition or deletion of chromosomes, in a procreative advantageous way, to lead to new types of organisms. Yet it is still more complicated than that.

Having 46 chromosomes does not make a human, as it could equally be a muntjac deer or a parhyale hawaiensis (a tiny crustacean, just a few millimetres in length, that resembles a shrimp). So, if a human child was born with 48 chromosomes, he/she would still be a human and not a gorilla, albeit with some serious medical conditions. In fact, Down's syndrome is an example of having 47 chromosomes and Turner Syndrome in women is an example of having only 45 chromosomes (missing a second X chromosome). Clearly, neither of these conditions is a genetic advantage. Similarly, if a gorilla gave birth to a baby with 46 chromosomes (possibly by a theorised mechanism of chromosome fusion), it would still be a gorilla and not a human.

To wrap it up, evolution requires both randomly occurring reproductive errors where offspring occur with abnormal chromosome numbers and randomly occurring mistakes in genetic code (replication error or acquired damage), such that they yield procreative advantage to win in Natural Selection. And, if enough of this occurs, a new, more complex and talented organism is born. This is the 'constructive mutations' element of the theory of evolution. Now for Natural Selection.

Natural Selection:

This is what I would call the plausible side of the theory of evolution, but it still causes problems for the theory. Simply put, Natural Selection (or Survival of the Fittest) suggests that the organism best suited to survive and procreate in the existing environment will carry on while the organisms least suited will die out. A frequent example in textbooks is the peppered moth, dark and light types. In less polluted areas the light type flourishes while in polluted cities or darker forests, the dark type flourishes. This is explained as the type more easily spotted by predators (birds) will have less chance to procreate and so decline in numbers. Apparently, prior to the industrial revolution, there was predominantly the light type, and then in the industrial revolution this shifted to black type predominance. With post industrial revolution improvements in air quality, the light type saw a resurgence. This is touted as evidence of evolution, but in fact it is has nothing to do with mutations and is only an example of natural selection as both light and dark type were in existence all along. There were no genetic changes, only population changes.

A similar example would be red and grey squirrels, where grey squirrels have prospered and are causing the decline of red squirrel populations. There are several factors associated with this, but basically the grey squirrel seems to be the fittest at this time, so it survives. Again, this is not an example of evolution, but rather natural selection.

However, there are some problems with natural selection as it applies to evolution. First, natural selection does not necessarily favour the more advanced, more complex, more capable or more intelligent versions of an organism, but rather it favours the ones that procreate the most, which also favours the ones that live longer so have more time for procreation. Hence, from an evolutionary standpoint the world should be full of very robust organisms that have great resistance to climate change, have very flexible dietary requirements, are very resistant to predators and have highly successful immune systems, and most of all, are great reproducers. This does not seem to support the animal kingdom that we see in our world today, especially in light of the great number of endangered species that we see, along with those already extinct. It seems more consistent with a world of cockroaches!

Secondly, natural selection favours the normal rather than the abnormal where choice is concerned, or the more aggressive or powerful where less choice is concerned. In most species, the abnormal are less desirable for mating partners, so less likely to mate where partners have choice. Mutations, by definition, are abnormal. They are the extremes or outliers that are less favoured and more likely to die out. The idea that random mutations occur giving rise to a new form of an organism, a one off, an oddball, and that this new form procreates to continue this oddity to the point of causing the decline of the normal sounds very attractive, but not very consistent with natural selection. Rather, it is wholly consistent with artificial selection, ie breeding.

Now, having considered how evolution is supposed to work, let's consider why it doesn't.

Chapter 6 The Case Against Evolution

Evolution is an attractive theory, but as we have seen, it rests on evidence that is circumstantial and not on that which is theoretical, or even empirical. Various primates have great similarities with humans, both in appearance and in genetics, and we know that mutations and changes in the gene pool take place and that natural selection occurs, hence the circumstantial evidence. However, when held up to the scrutiny of Scientific principles, the theory of Evolution crumbles. The principles we will consider are as follows:

- Mutations are errors, and are destructive rather than constructive
- Entropy must increase / complexity must decrease
- Irreducible complexity and sequencing
- The opposition of Natural Selection
- Mendel's Peas and boundaries between species
- Absence of fossil evidence, Burgess Shale
- Human races, pygmies, giants, patriarch ages, language and more

Mutations:

When I was at University, (this is about to show my age!), I was taught Fortran programming on a mainframe computer. We would write out our program and then keypunch each line onto a card, creating a large stack of keypunched cards which would then be fed into the computer by a technician. An hour or so later, you would get a printout of your program and results. If there was one mistake on any card, or a single card missing, your program would fail or give incorrect results. Faults in the program were destructive. This is the problem with mutations.

Mutations are, by definition, random changes in the structure of a gene, and they are caused by random, destructive processes. In fact, the definition reads 'the changing in the structure of a gene...caused by the alteration of single base units in DNA, or the deletion, insertion or rearrangement of larger sections of genes or chromosomes'. The key is the randomness of mutations required by the evolutionary model. In the very recent development of gene therapy and genetic modification, a directed, not random, process is used (requiring the input of information), and thus it can be constructive. However, the randomness of mutations in nature lacks direction or information input and as a result is always destructive, corrupting the pre-mutated order. A common example sited as a constructive mutation is sickle-cell anaemia, resulting in immunity to malaria. This is clearly not a constructive change, despite the side effect of malaria resistance, as it is a condition that reduces the oxygen carrying capacity of the blood leading to various health problems and shortening average lifespan to the mid-forties (according to studies done in the early 1980s).

Another common example mentioned is the ability of bacteria to append genetic strands into their code, thus altering their genetic makeup and 'adapting' to their environment, such as developing antibiotic resistant strains of diseases (superbugs). This is a feature specific to bacteria, and possibly some other single-celled organisms. It does not involve the creation of new genetic code (just adding on pre-existing code), it does not result in bacteria evolving into non-bacterial organisms and it does not take place in more complex organisms such as animals.

Furthermore, the processes behind mutations in nature, as discussed previously (replication errors or environmentally induced molecular damage), are destructive processes. In fact, from generation to generation, we are increasing the number of 'faults' in our genes resulting in an overall decline in the quality of the human gene pool. This will be discussed later as 'devolution'.

Entropy:

As discussed earlier in The Second Law of Thermodynamics, entropy must increase in all natural processes. Entropy is disorder or randomness or reduction in complexity. Entropy in a specific context can increase, but only with the input of energy and information. For example, I can erect a shed by assembling a random pile of building materials into an ordered arrangement with walls and a door, thereby increasing the order of that system. However, I had to eat and burn calories to 'erect' the structure and those digestive and respirative processes caused a much larger decrease in order than the increase of the ordered structure of the shed, resulting in an overall increase in disorder, or entropy. Additionally, I had to input my intent (information) in erecting the materials into a specific pattern, hence the requirement of energy **and information** to increase the order or complexity of the specific system of the shed.

Likewise, for evolution, the second law of thermodynamics cannot be broken, hence entropy, disorder, must increase. However, the theory of evolution suggests exactly the opposite. It suggests that very simple organisms of very low complexity have evolved, through natural processes, into highly complex organisms. They use the shed idea that this reverse in entropy can occur using the energy input from the sun, **but there is no input of information**. There is no intent or direction in the process as the mutations are random, natural events. Theistic evolution would be a possible solution to this problem as God could supernaturally supply the intent / direction in the mutations (divine genetic modification), but this defeats the 'natural' aspect of evolution.

Even more is the problem of going from a chemical soup to the simple organisms in the first place (Biogenesis), which also requires a giant increase in order and complexity, again lacking intent or direction (which has been discussed in the section on the beginning of life). Essentially we have a theory in direct conflict with a basic physical law of the universe. The second law of thermodynamics stands, and the theory of evolution must fall.

Irreducible Complexity:

In the debate over evolution, the argument of irreducible complexity frequently comes up. Irreducible complexity is the idea that certain organs (eg. the eye) or certain structures (eg. the flagellum) involve a complexity of parts and assembly that exclude any possible sequence of evolutionary steps for its development. Evolution suggests a mutation causes a change in the organism, which thrives due to natural selection until the next mutation, etc, leading through a number of steps into the current model of the organism, but the eye is a very complex structure that is either complete or dysfunctional; there is no **stepwise process** to evolve it. In other words, there is no rational sequence of steps to evolve a human eye from a more primitive eye or sensory organ. From whatever starting point until the fully functioning eye, all the steps of the process would involve useless structures with no environmental advantage to be preserved by natural selection.

The problem is not just evolving the parts, but at the same time a sequence of construction. Imagine an electric shaver. You could have all the parts and materials to make the shaver, but if they are not assembled in the correct sequence, it cannot be made to function. So it is with most human organs. It is not just a matter of evolving the various tissues and elements of an organ, but the sequence and mechanism of construction, in the womb, must also be evolved. Any genetic deviation (mutation), for it to be successful, must not only code for the new or altered part, but also for an effective sequence of construction of that part, and of that part into the whole. Evolving a Boeing 747 airplane would not simply involve starting with a simple flying machine and then building a better one, then better still, and so forth until building the

747. Rather, evolving the 747 would involve starting with a simple flying machine and then changing a part at a time to result in a better flying machine, and so forth until a 747 is formed. That would not be possible, and even more so is it impossible to evolve a human from a simpler living organism.

I won't discuss the Irreducible Complexity argument further here, as it is readily expounded elsewhere in far better detail and clarity (ie. Google it!). Suffice it to say that it strongly refutes the plausibility of evolution.

Natural Selection's Opposition:

Natural selection is all to do with successful reproduction. Survival of the fittest means survival of the members of a specie that are effective reproducers, live long enough to effectively reproduce and are most successful at attracting a mate (where applicable) to be able to reproduce. It does not, for example, favour greater intelligence unless that intelligence enables it to live longer for a longer reproducing period or unless that intelligence made it more attractive to a mate. In some contexts, greater strength is advantageous as it enables a member to resist others and claim a mate for itself, such as a male lion taking over a pride. So in particular contexts, certain features will be naturally selected, but in general, natural selection eliminates oddballs.

Evolution is all about mutations producing oddballs, which end up becoming the new norm until the next evolutionary step. But natural selection is all about eliminating those oddballs unless they are better reproducers, for whatever reason. And this isn't just about a mutation resulting in a person having six fingers and the probability of that person finding a mate being reduced, but it is about crossing genetic boundaries (increasing or decreasing chromosome numbers) and becoming particularly odd, thereby reducing its probability of successfully mating. Where evolution requires oddballs, natural selection eliminates them.

Mendel's Peas:

This isn't as much an argument as a curiosity to me. In Biology textbooks everywhere, Gregor Mendel is recognised as the founder of modern genetics, largely to do with his work with Pea plants. He came up with some basic rules of genetics which we hold to today, and one of those most basic rules is that organisms reproduce in kind. A pea plant will only reproduce into a pea plant. A dog will only produce a dog. There are boundaries between organisms and things don't reproduce across

The Rational Choice

those boundaries (typically recognised as species). However, just a few pages along in those textbooks, evolution will be expounded in which organisms reproduced to form new organisms, crossing those fixed boundaries. In all genetic research to date, I don't know of any example of natural crossing of these genetic boundaries. Peas still only produce peas; the law is true. Yet the theory of evolution breaks the law of reproducing in kind.

Fossil Evidence and the Burgess Shale:

Cars are an example of something that we might say have 'evolved' over time (using the term in a general rather than scientific sense). There are many cars from the 1980s still around to be seen, fewer from the 1960s, fewer still from the 1940s and still fewer from the 1920s. From their conception, newer, better models were developed from one decade to the next, and the evidence of earlier models decreases the further back you look in time. There is nothing 'natural' about this, but I am using this example to illustrate the issue with fossil evidence.

Evolution says that through mutations, better versions develop and thrive and outlast the earlier versions, and this process continues even to today. Therefore, it would make sense that the fossil evidence would be rich in more recent versions, and this would decline as you look back in time to earlier stages of evolution. Equally, the progressive stages of evolutionary progress should be seen in the fossil evidence (ie. more abundance of the more recent stages and less abundance of the earlier stages). There should be an abundance of 'missing links' rather than the headline news every 10 or 20 years of a new missing link being discovered, which inevitably turns out to be confirmed to be a gibbon or a malnourished human or a hoax. And this should be true across all current animal species, not just humans. In reality, there are fossils of humans and gibbons and nothing in-between; and there are fossils of modern dogs and ancient dogs but nothing in-between. There are fish gills and the appearance of lines in mammal embryo scans which were used to suggest an evolutionary link, but this was shown to be complete nonsense. Where are the fossils?

In addition to this is the problem of the 'missing links' that are proposed from time to time. When you read on from the initial headlines and first few paragraphs, these finds inevitably turn out to be a tooth, or a piece of a jaw bone from which an overly creative mind construes a whole creature including its size, features, intellect and lifestyle. Accuse me of scepticism, but I find that the headlines of 'Missing Link Found' and 'Evidence of Life Found on Mars' are not worth the paper (or cyberspace) they are written on.

Back in the 1990s I was handed a book on The Burgess Shale by Stephen Jay Gould as a fascinating read supporting evolution, from fossil evidence. The book, and the finds described were fascinating, however it did not provide any evidence for evolution. The writer, S J Gould, was himself an evolutionist, so he interpreted his finds though his mindset of evolution to suggest a tree-like diagram of primordial life evolving into a multitude of species of organisms, most of which were made extinct through various environmental shifts in the earth's history or cataclysmic events such as a giant asteroid collision, like that suggested for the extinction of dinosaurs. So he constructed a tree, with branches pruned throughout the tree, but with more branches continually sprouting. This brings us to the present time with all the varieties of organisms we have today being only a small fraction of the plethora of types of organisms that have existed in the past. However, his data consists of two points: 1. At the time of the deposition of the Burgess Shale there was a broad range of organisms, most of which we do not have today; and 2. Today's range of organisms is much more limited. As an evolutionist, he proposed this tree model of new varieties of organisms constantly sprouting while other varieties were cut off, but equally, if not preferably, this data supports the creationist model of God creating a vast range of organisms to start with and through extinctions the range in varieties has diminished to what we see today.

Chapter 7 Other Thoughts

Human Races

In January of 1988, Newsweek magazine ran a front-page headline of 'The Search for Adam & Eve' (I still have a copy of this issue). The article is to do with research indicating that every woman alive (and thus every person) can be linked back to a common ancestor, an Eve, through mitochondrial DNA. I also have an article cut out from the Daily Mail newspaper (circa 2000 I think, written by Natasha Courtenay-Smith) citing research from Professor Bryan Sykes of Oxford University which confirms this common ancestor claim from mitochondrial DNA, estimating this ancestor to have lived in Africa 150,000 years ago. In fact, this Daily Mail article suggests that every woman in the world can be traced back to 36 'clan mothers', which in turn trace back to the common Eve, and that 41% of Europeans are descended from one of these 36 clan mothers, whom they have named Helena. The breakdown of these 36 is fascinating; 13 colonised Africa, 4 colonised America, 7 colonised Europe and the remaining 12 colonised the Asian countries; and these 36 were to have lived between 8,000 and 50,000 years ago.

This evidence doesn't particularly disprove either Creationism or Evolutionary Theory, as it can be interpreted to support either. Clearly Creationists would refer this original mother to the first woman created, Eve, and deduce that all subsequent humans are descended from her. On the other hand, Evolutionists would say that all humans living today have been bred into her line, and that all other human lines were inferior to Eve's, or unlucky, and thus died out.

However, these 36 clan mothers do give a valuable insight into racial development. Essentially, from one woman, and man, came these 36 different and distinct women. This would include skin colour, size, hair and other distinguishing features. That is not to say that these 36 women necessarily all looked different, but they had sufficiently unique genetic blueprints to develop into the various races we see around the globe. Bottom line; we are all descended from the same original mother, and that is what Creationism predicts.

Pygmies

I grew up mainly in the 1960s and 1970s, in the state of New York, USA, on a diet of National Geographic magazine and evolution. Apparently, it wasn't illegal to teach creationism, but it wasn't in the textbooks, and it was considered religion, not science, hence kept out of schools. Therefore, I was taught, and indoctrinated into evolutionary thinking. When I read National Geographic articles studying South American pygmies, I subconsciously started to perceive them as an almost sub-human specie. It was almost like looking at them in the zoo. It was only 15 to 20 years later, when first challenged with the science behind Creationism, that I started to perceive my own subconscious beliefs in this matter, essentially a form of racism. It was a simple step to take evolutionary teaching of evolving from lower to higher organisms, and the zoo-like study of a very distinctly different race with an apparent absence of technological and intellectual development, and form a belief that this race is a step lower on the evolutionary ladder. This thinking is clearly wrong, and I cannot say that it was ever explicitly taught to me, but I would suggest that it could, and did, follow logically from my education. It wasn't helped by the fact that the suburbia I grew up in had very little racial diversity, so I had very little experience of other racial groups.

From a Creationist view, or from the '36 clan mothers' perspective, it is easy to see the equality of all races, as well as the way that races and tribes and variations in technological progress developed. Interestingly, where people groups or tribes develop through several generations in isolation from other groups, it seems to me that they not only develop technology more slowly, but that they actually regress technologically to the basics of survival. And, I believe this happens with language as well, as will be discussed later in this chapter. So, basically, the Pygmies of South America are a race of people who have been isolated for so many generations that they are unique in their language and absence of technology, but equal in their humanity and value. They too are descendants of Eve.

Giants

The Bible's most renown giant was Goliath, nearly 10 ft tall, who was slain by David, the shepherd boy/young man. But there were many other 'giants' noted, both before and after the flood. As to the extent of fossil evidence of giants, there are plenty of books referring to such evidence, but an absence of reputable, evolutionary biased, sources such as the Smithsonian reporting of giants. Regardless, the existence of giants in the past, does not disprove either Creationism or Evolutionary Theory. In both cases, giant races could have developed through the original genetics of Eve (just as the Pygmy have), or through a separate evolutionary path (evolution only). However, the gene alleles responsible for the exceptional growth do seem to be absent from our present-day gene pool indicating that those carrying them have died out.

This leads to a particular idea of mine which I will refer to as genetic potential. (See footnote at end of this chapter.) Dogs have been bred for centuries to produce a huge range of characteristics illustrated by the Dachshund (sausage dog), the Whippet and the Great Dane. Essentially, they are bred from a general dog centuries back through selective breeding. But you could not take a pair of Great Danes now, and selectively breed them, regardless of how many generations, to produce a Dachshund. In other words, the general dog centuries ago had a large genetic potential, resulting in the multitude of breeds today, but a modern-day purebred has a much more limited genetic potential, being able to be bred into just a narrow range of characteristics. Similarly, the first man and woman, Adam and Eve, would have had a very large genetic potential resulting in all the races and sizes of people we have today, but if you chose a couple from today's population, you would be much more limited on the downstream races and sizes that could develop. Therefore, as a Creationist, I would say that the first Adam and Eve had a very great genetic potential and that this genetic potential has decreased through the generations as certain genes, or gene alleles, are lost through races dying out, such as the giants.

This causes a problem for evolution as a high genetic potential in humans should not have formed in the first place, as humans would have been a very special, unique result of mutation and thus similar in a sense to a very unique breed of dog with low genetic potential. The only explanations of high genetic potential (needed to explain today's racial variety) would be divine creation or separately evolved strands of humanity cross breeding, which potentially leads back to racism.

> *As an aside: One final point on giants is the Biblical reference to Nephilim. In the Bible, Genesis chapter 6 verses 1-8, it refers to the 'Sons of God' having relations with the 'daughters of men' and producing children who were the 'heroes of old, men of renown'. This led, in the narrative, directly into the wickedness of mankind and the need for God to send the flood to cleanse the earth of this wickedness. The Nephilim are thus seen as evil, and also (post-flood) as giants occupying the 'promised land' prior to the Israelite invasion. Many Christians (and Jews?) would interpret the 'Sons of God' to be angels and the Nephilim to be an evil race carrying a corrupted gene pool (mixed human and angel). This then necessitated the flood, to stop the "pandemic" of this corrupted gene pool with its inherent evil. Yet, some of these*

corrupted genes were carried forward by one of the wives of Noah's three sons, leading to the giants in the promised land. This then gives a possible explanation for the command to Joshua to kill every man, woman, and child as they invaded the promised land, which has otherwise been difficult for Christians to reconcile with our loving God. I've included this comment on the Nephilim while addressing this topic of giants, but it is not particularly relevant to the Creation-Evolution discussion of this section.

Patriarch Ages

To repeat, the theory of evolution suggests that all the organisms and species we see today, and a host of extinct organisms as seen in the Burgess Shale, all have evolved from simple organisms far back in time. It would involve mutations and natural selection to produce enhanced versions of an organism until finally, through more extreme mutations a new organism is formed with a different number of chromosomes. It is analogous to the advancement of motor cars from the model T to a modern Jaguar (still internal combustion, drive chain vehicles) followed by a leap to jet vehicles of some futuristic type like in the movie The Fifth Element. However, what we actually see in thousands of years of history, fossil evidence, and modern genetic research is the slow deterioration within a specie until it becomes extinct, with no crossing of boundaries to a new organism or specie. This is what I refer to as devolution.

Taking humans as an example, we would start with a perfect set of 23 chromosome pairs (46 chromosomes). Through environmental damage such as cosmic rays and background radioactive emissions from our environment, and through replication errors in forming the reproductive gametes or in subsequent stem cells, the subsequent generations will have defects in their chromosomes. These defects will, for the most part, be insignificant as far as the outward expression of the genes because of the incredible checks and balances within our genetic makeup that correct for a large number of faults. None-the-less, the faults will gradually increase from generation to generation. Where a population is isolated, the accumulation of faults will increase more rapidly as both parents are more likely to share the same faults increasing the probability of passing them on. Where there is more mixing of populations, faults can be lost but the overall trend is still an increase in these genetic faults. Therefore, contrary to evolution and the continual march towards enhanced versions, the reality is a downward spiral into deteriorating genes, which can be slowed through mixing of gene pools (mixing of ethnicities and worldwide populations) but cannot be halted or reversed. Devolution of our genes down the generations is inevitable.

Scientifically, this devolution trend is wholly inconsistent with the theory of evolution, but it is completely consistent with Creationism. If God created the first man (as well as every other specie ever in existence), then the first man, and woman, would have had perfect genes, and in fact, would have lived a very long life as it is the deterioration in our genes that accelerates the aging process. Their children could mate with one another (what we now call incest) without any birth defects, mental or physical, as they would not have matching genetic faults which would combine to the detriment of the offspring. In dogs we see this constantly played out when the breeders use dogs of close relation resulting in the classic health problems of specific breeds (eg. back problems with Dachshunds). What we would see is perfect physical specimens with long life spans and no inherent physical problems slowly deteriorating over hundreds, and possibly thousands of generations to shorter life spans and a host of physical issues.

One of the seemingly preposterous claims in the Bible is the genealogy of the patriarchs found in Genesis chapter 5. Starting with the first man, Adam, the patriarchs are listed with lifespans in the 900 years range, the longest being Methuselah with 969 years. Following the flood, and Noah with 950 years, the lifespans rapidly decrease to 600 (Shem), to the 400s (Arphaxad, Shelah, Eber), to the 200s (Peleg, Reu, Serug, Terah), and then 175 years with Abraham. There are two significant drops in that sequence coming after Noah (after the flood) and during Peleg ('in his time the Earth was divided', Genesis 10:25). The first drop (900's to 400's) came after the flood and the second (400's to 200's) came when 'the Earth was divided'. The Bible indicates that the worldwide flood waters came partly from underground and partly from the heavens or upper atmosphere ('the springs of the great deep burst forth, and the floodgates of the heavens were opened', Genesis 7:11). It is believed there was a great canopy of water vapour in the upper atmosphere producing a greenhouse around the whole Earth and shielding the Earth from damaging cosmic rays, primarily from the sun. With the collapse of this canopy in producing the 40 days and nights of continuous rain everywhere, people were subject to a greater rate of genetic damage through these cosmic rays which may have contributed to this first lifespan drop. The second drop during the time of Peleg seems to be related to the Earth being divided. Was there a catastrophic breaking up of the Pangaea at this time which has slowed to what we now see as continental drift? It is not clear, but in a relatively short time lifespans seemed to nearly halve. Another 600 years after Abraham we have Moses living to the age of 120 years but writing in a Psalm that man is given a lifespan of 70 or 80 years (Psalm 90).

It is also of note to consider the role of incest from our modern genetic perspective. Starting with Adam and Eve, incest was a necessity, their children had to mate with one another, **but there was nothing wrong with it.** They had perfect genes and there was no threat to their offspring. This principle continues right through the patriarchs to Noah with no notable change in lifespan. In fact, incest continues as a normal practice right up to Abraham, whose wife, Sarah, was his half-sister. It is 600 years later, when Moses is given the Law from God, that incest is proclaimed wrong. Sometime during those 600 years, incest ceased to be acceptable, and safe for the offspring, and it became recognised as unsafe and even wrong. Clearly, the deteriorating quality of mankind's genes, through the generations, had caused incest to change from safe and normal to unsafe and wrong. Possibly this was a significant factor in the two lifespan drops discussed in the last paragraph. None-the-less, we can see how genetic devolution within mankind is fully consistent with the Biblical record and with Creationism.

Language

Language is unique to humans. Other creatures communicate, sometimes with greater sophistication such as dolphins or whales, but nowhere near the level of language. Humans are unique in both their physiology and intelligence in being capable of language, and all humans have that same essential capability unless it has been lost through mental or physical impairment of some kind. In fact, it is largely this unique capability of language that establishes the gulf between mankind and all other living creatures. Once more we are faced with the incapability of the theory of evolution to supply any plausible mechanism for crossing this gulf. It is not a single step, but an incredible leap in both physiology and intelligence, and it only seems to have taken place, from an evolutionist's perspective, in the one chain from chimpanzee to human. If possible once, why hasn't it happened in other animals? Basically, evolution cannot explain the existence of language.

In contrast to this, Creationism supports language. God created mankind with the capability for language as well as a language to start with. In Genesis 2 and 3 there are actual dialogues recorded between God and Adam/Eve and Satan and Eve, and Adam fulfilled his task of naming all the animals and his wife, Eve. Moses is generally credited with authoring the first 5 books of the Bible, but clearly the whole book of Genesis predates Moses, so it would have had to have been passed on to him in a language, and most likely written in some form for Moses to compile the accounts into one. Equally, the first 3 or 4 chapters of Genesis would have had to have been passed on from Adam himself. In creation, God imbued mankind with a language from the start.

The Bible goes on to record that the whole world had one language, both before and after the flood, but that a common language drew mankind together into a humanistic centre rather than venturing out and filling the earth, as God had commanded. So, God 'confused their languages', supernaturally imbuing the various groups of people with different languages so that they were unable to understand one another and therefore moved apart (Tower of Babel in Genesis 11). Having spread out, through what may have still been a Pangaea, or supercontinent, they were then cast out into separate continents during the time of Peleg when the earth was divided. I must add that this idea of a Pangaea being broken up during the time of Peleg is my own idea, stemming from the single phrase, 'in his time the earth was divided' found in Genesis 10:25. (See footnote at end of this chapter.)

Suddenly, there is a plethora of different languages, of seemingly different starting points rather than being derived from a single language, and this is what we see today. There are reported to be up to 140 language families around the globe giving rise to over 7000 languages.

> *Another aside: It seems to me, that based on evolution, homo sapiens, once evolved, would have rapidly developed a common language while still a single community, resulting in one starting point. To arrive at 140 language families suggests 140 distinct starting points, which would suggest 140 separately evolved communities, or 140 different races which, in this context, would not be equal because they evolved separately. Another point where evolution could support racism.*

Further to this is the complexity of languages. Where people are more concentrated and organised, there can be language development, somewhat like what we see in technological development. Where people are spread out or not well organised as a country (eg. tribal societies), there is little if any language development, but rather language deterioration. The working vocabulary decreases and the language syntax greatly simplifies. It is easy to see how the language of an isolated community would rapidly deteriorate. It is also easy to see how technology has developed over time, however, it is not as easy to see how complex languages could have developed over time. Clearly, vocabulary is constantly being added to our language, but syntax of the spoken language is always being pulled downwards towards simplicity rather than towards greater complexity. Where has language come from and where did the complexity of language, both modern and ancient, come from? I find it very hard to believe that it has developed from the grunts of prehistoric man as evolution would have it. Rather, it makes more sense to me that we were given language at creation, with its complex structure, and it is vocabulary that has developed since.

Cavemen, Intelligence and Devolution

This puzzle of language naturally leads on to the discussion of cavemen. Once again, evolution has given us this mindset of primitive man, cavemen, with apelike appearance and grunting for communication, and having a lower form of intelligence, somewhere between chimpanzee and modern man. Of course, there is no evidence of this, only the evidence of primitive technology (not unlike that of primitive tribes today). Would this suggest that more primitive tribespeople of today are in fact a few steps lower on the evolutionary ladder with a lower intelligence as well, because they have primitive technology? We all know this is wrong, but isn't this what an evolutionary mindset would indicate? Equally, the impression of Neanderthal man is that they were an earlier step, or sidestep, of the evolutionary ladder with lower intelligence, but the evidence is only of lower technology. Fortunately, modern ideas seem to be shifting towards Neanderthals being the same as modern man, just another ethnicity which has, for the most part, died out.

From a creationist's view, mankind has always been fully intelligent, and cavemen and Neanderthals had language and intelligence equal to (maybe even better than) that of today. They started with no technology. The first man and woman are reported to have made their first clothes out of fig leaves, and then God made them clothes from animal skins, that is the start of technology. By the 7th generation from Adam, we have it recorded that there was Jabal (father of those who live in tents and raise livestock), his brother Jubal (father of those who play the harp and flute), and half-brother, Tubal-Cain (who forged tools from bronze and iron) - Genesis 4: 19-22. We see the progression of technology, which one could argue was very slow from Tubal-Cain up to the printing press of the 1400s, where technological development was built upon that which came before (standing on the shoulders of those who came before us). Then, with the printing press and the preservation, sharing and dissemination of knowledge, technological development began its near exponential increase which we see continuing today. So clearly technological prowess is not a measure of intelligence, but rather a progression of ideas and capabilities. There is nothing to suggest people of the past were less intelligent, even going back to cavemen and Neanderthals. Instead, might they have been more intelligent?

As was previously explained, the human genetic pool is slowly deteriorating due to increasing genetic damage from generation to generation. With the huge increase in travel and ethnic mixing, this deterioration has almost stopped, or possibly reversed temporarily, but it basically follows a relentless downward pull, like that of gravity. So, since we are genetically slightly inferior to our ancestors, particularly ancient ancestors, is it possible that our intelligence is also slightly inferior? Were Neanderthals more intelligent than modern man? It is an interesting question.

One final word on technology and 'primitive' people. It seems to me that when people groups become more isolated, technology goes backwards. Hence technological backwardness could be seen as regression or stagnation from a point where the people group became isolated from other populations. Just imagine a post-apocalyptic scenario where survivors band together to rebuild society, but they lack all the infrastructure to support our modern technology. Within one or two generations I could imagine us back to the technology of the industrial revolution, but having the memory of what could be developed. How long before we could re-invent and build a mobile phone?

Footnote: Throughout this section I have expressed many ideas that are mine, and I am not trying to imply that these ideas are widely held by Creationists in general, nor am I now saying they are not widely held. They are my ideas (I have not read them elsewhere), but that is not to say that they are not also expressed by others that I am not aware of.

Chapter 8 The Case for Evolution

Perhaps the strongest case against evolution is the case for evolution. It starts with Darwin observing and documenting the remarkable differences between populations of the same specie having unique characteristics which are related to their survival in the habitat they occupy. A long beaked variety thrives in one habitat where a short beaked variety thrives in a different habitat. Darwin suggested a mechanism of natural selection by which small inherited changes could lead to large differences many generations later. From this came the expression that the long beaked variety adapted to their environment, and somewhere along the line the word mutations slipped in, to somehow account for bigger changes. The confusion starts with the fact that mutations had nothing to do with it. From an original bird pair there was a variety of beak lengths. Those with longer beaks in the one habitat survived better and prospered, to the exclusion of the shorter beaked ones. This advantage of beak length always favoured the longer ones, so beak lengths increased from generation to generation (much as height in people seems to be increasing in some countries) until they were all longer beaked. A similar trend may have occurred in the short beak habitat. Essentially, no mutations were involved, just natural selection. Although it may just be seen as semantics, the birds didn't evolve or adapt to suit their environment; those that survived were better suited and prospered. There was no creation of new or inherently different genetic coding, just selection of the favoured coding.

The point is that natural selection leads to the potential for substantial diversification within a specie, but it does not lead to a genetically new specie. We see that with people, and the wonderful variation in populations around the globe, and we see it with dogs and artificial selection, breeding, to produce hundreds of unique breeds, but they are still dogs.

The other evidence for evolution is circumstantial; there is so much similarity between living creatures. Some primates look so much like people, abounding in physical similarities from joints and bone structure to anatomy and movement. Then there are the genetic similarities as well, suggesting that humans and chimpanzees share between 96% to 99% of our DNA, while we share around 85% of our DNA with dogs, etc. My house may share 98% of its construction materials with those of a tower block in London, but it doesn't mean that one came out of the other. These similarities do not imply that people evolved from primates, but rather that people and primates are formed from the same materials and with similar design features. This suggests a common creator, not evolution.

So, the evidence for evolution can be summed up quite simply as the physical and genetic commonality between organisms, and Natural Selection as a mechanism. The former better supports a common creator, and the latter explains the diversity seen in this world, but not its evolution.

Chapter 9 The Conclusion of the Matter

So here is the conclusion of the matter. We exist in a universe that had a beginning and required something else, pre-existent, from which it came. The atheist view has no plausible explanation for this, much less any evidence. A God, of omnipotence and omniscience is a plausible explanation, even though such a God is beyond our comprehension.

The physical laws of our universe, principally the second law of thermodynamics, require that order cannot come out of disorder, but rather that order had to come first. Hence created order at the beginning is necessary rather than an evolution from disorder to order. The Big Bang had to be programmed, not random, and all living things had to be created (order first), rather than evolved (disorder first).

Living organisms are so incredibly complicated, and involve structures, processes and constructive sequences (forming in the womb), that they could not form from any process of random change (mutations), regardless of time and Natural Selection; not even the most simple forms of living creatures. The beginning of life has no, remotely plausible, naturalistic explanation; it requires a supernatural explanation, a creative event.

Finally, the theory of evolution, the bastion of atheistic argument, does not work. It is not consistent with the nature of mutations (faults); it is not consistent with the physical laws of the universe (2nd law of thermodynamics); it is not consistent with the existence of complex, irreducible organs or structures; it is not consistent with the normalising effect of natural selection; it is not consistent with our understanding of genetics and reproduction in kind; and it is not consistent with the fossil evidence (or the lack of fossil evidence). Additionally, evolutionary thought lends itself to racism and ethnic supremacy doctrines that are morally bankrupt. The theory, from the mid-1800s, is wrong. Our existence, as humans, requires a creator.

All of the above cries out, "there must be a God", and that God must be omnipotent, omniscient and a lot of other things to have created everything, including us. The next section of this book is about who that God must be and what religious belief is the truth.

The Rational Choice

Part 2: Why Christianity

The Rational Choice

Chapter 1 Seeking the Truth

At the trial of Jesus before the Roman Governor - Pontius Pilate, Jesus claimed that He came into this world to testify to the truth. Pilate responded, hypothetically I believe, 'What is truth?'. Things haven't changed much in the last 2000 years as, today, truth seems to be very subjective, "you have your truth and I have my truth", however, I don't ascribe to this. We may all have our own perspective on things (like viewing an elephant from different angles), but there usually is an underlying truth to most matters, and that is definitely my belief when it comes to religion and spiritual beliefs.

A few years ago, a tumultuous event took place in Washington DC; a group of protesters, supporting Donald Trump in claiming an unfair and stolen election, stormed the congress building, and interrupted the process of ratifying the election results which made Joe Biden the next president of the USA. I was shocked, my family was shocked, and the nation was shocked. In fact, many around the world were shocked. What is more, I was shocked by the contrasting views, or more appropriately, beliefs, that were being expressed (within my own family as well as across the nation):

- Trump is a great man, a great leader, a true patriot, a truthful man who tells it like it is, a true supporter of democracy and the US constitution; there was serious election fraud resulting in a stolen election by the liberals/democrats; there is a wealth of evidence to prove this; the entire media apart from a very few select TV and radio stations are controlled by this liberal/democrat philosophy; much of the nation is being duped by the fake news of this biased and deluded media

- Trump is a corrupt man, a self-promoter, a power and attention seeking individual, a dictator by nature, a liar and manipulator, a ruthless leader who vilifies those who oppose him, a threat to the constitution and to democracy; there was no significant election fraud in the free and fair election; the election of Joe Biden is valid and there is no reasonable evidence to the contrary; there are just a few right-wing TV and radio stations broadcasting biased propaganda while most of the media is generally reliable

While necessarily oversimplified, these two views represented the two opposing beliefs in my family, and to some extent, in the American nation, and these beliefs were forged and reinforced by the particular media being followed. Each belief had a narrative that had been adopted, and was held to, as an underlying truth. Hence, I refer to these two positions as beliefs, or faiths, rather than views as they formed a framework for interpreting information rather than a perspective that could be informed and altered by additional information. These beliefs / faiths are strongly held to, regardless of the evidence, because the 'evidence' is either re-interpreted to support the chosen belief or disregarded as false or unreliable. In January 2024, (3 years after the storming of the Congress building) with Donald Trump facing various upcoming court cases for insurrection, obstruction of leadership transition, attempted election tampering, etc., it seemed most people still held to their belief – despite the wealth of evidence disproving any election fraud and disproving the rhetoric of the Trump camp. By April 2024, Donald Trump had won the Republican Presidential candidate nomination. And as you read this, you will already know what transpired at the end of May 2024 and beyond.

The point here is that the American public became strongly divided over a few fundamental beliefs such as Big Government?, Social Responsibility?, Free Market? and Individual Freedoms?, and then, with the help of the media and individuals such as Donald Trump, and certainly others on the Democrat side, the two sides became so deeply entrenched in their beliefs and the resulting narratives that truth, understanding and reason got lost.

Well, this is the situation faced in this section of the book. We all have beliefs about our existence which are generally codified in the multitude of religions around the world or in a bespoke faith such as scientific atheism (no god, no purpose, just a product of random chance). These beliefs form our framework from which to interpret our world and experience (the evidence), and as a result, they are more strongly held to, the longer we have them. We form a narrative around our belief which is reinforced and refined through sources consistent with our belief, and we disregard or re-interpret sources that are not consistent with our belief. This is what we, people, do.

So, in this section, I am presenting evidence which may challenge your narrative, possibly your belief itself if you are not already a Christian, and I am asking you to **try** to be open-minded enough to not disregard or re-interpret the evidence presented, but rather to consider where the evidence leads and be open enough to change. For me, when turning thirty, this process took nine months of daily conversations and debate over the 'evidence' to change my belief and begin a new narrative. Thereafter, as a Christian, the narrative around my belief has had to undergo a few revisions in the last 30 years, but that is good. That is the scientific model, to keep our belief and narrative sufficiently plastic to allow it to be revised as new evidence is presented. I don't mean carried by the wind, but sufficiently plastic to avoid rigid dogmatism.

Rarely, in our day to day lives, are we able to have a well-reasoned, well-educated discussion of what religion is the truth (including atheism as a religion in this context) for the following reasons: such conversations usually turn into debates, such conversations are too awkward, such conversations are not politically correct in public, such conversations cause offense, etc. As a result, we fail to reasonably deal with the most fundamental, and arguably most important question of our lives, "why?".

In this section, I will present some of the rationale/evidence behind the claim that the Christian faith is the truth, to the exclusion of all other religions and conflicting belief systems. I recognise that many readers may ask, "which Christian faith?", and I accept the validity of such a question, but I am referring to the basic, core Christian faith, outlined in the Bible, as follows:

- God is our creator
- God's nature is to love
- God is a trinity (Father, Son and Holy Spirit)
- Jesus is the incarnate Son of God, the fulness of God in bodily form

- Jesus willingly gave Himself, sacrificially unto death, as an atonement for all mankind and then was resurrected from death to eternal life
- "That God so loved the world, that He gave His only begotten Son, that whosoever believes in Him shall have eternal life"
- That Jesus Christ was the fulfilment of the Law and the Prophets of the Old Testament of the Bible

This is the core belief of Christianity which is common to all the central creeds of the faith and the three main branches of the church, Roman Catholic, Protestant and Eastern Orthodox, and it is the core message of the Bible. (See footnote regarding the Bible at the end of this chapter.)

The areas I will be discussing as evidence that Christianity is the one true faith are as follows:

- Beginnings – Is Christianity (the Bible) true in what it says about the origins of the universe, our world and mankind?
- Historical continuity and context – does Christianity show a logical continuity from the beginning of time until now, as opposed to springing up at some point in history with no roots back to the beginning?

- Purpose – does Christianity explain a purpose to our existence?
- Key People and Supernatural Events – who are the key people or fathers of the faith of Christianity and how were they confirmed by supernatural events to be evidence of the true faith?
- The Historical Jesus – who was Jesus and how was he confirmed to be the Christ, our Saviour, our God?
- Saved by Grace – what is Grace and how is it unique to Christianity?
- The Inner Witness (the Holy Spirit) – how is the Holy Spirit further confirmation of the truth?
- The big picture – how does the history of mankind all fit together from a Christian perspective?

So, let's start from where we left off at the end of Part 1, with the existence of God and a rational beginning.

Footnote (what is the Bible, in a nutshell?):

The Bible is the authoritative, foundational book of Christianity. It is comprised of the Old Testament (before Jesus was incarnate) and the New Testament (during Jesus ministry and thereafter). Both Testaments are collections of writings, called books, with the Old Testament containing 39 books and the

New Testament containing 27 books, for a total of 66 books. Both Testaments can be sub-divided as follows:

Old Testament:

- *Historical books – Genesis to Deuteronomy (the first 5 books called the Pentateuch and traditionally believed to be written by Moses), and Joshua to Esther (the next 12 books)*
- *Poetical books – Job to Song of Solomon (the next 5 books)*
- *Prophetical books – Isaiah to Malachi (the next 17 books) with the writing of Malachi finishing about 400 years prior to Jesus' birth*

New Testament:

- *Gospels and Acts – Matthew, Mark, Luke, John (the first 4 books describing Jesus' ministry) and the Acts of the Apostles (written by Luke, the writer of the Gospel, Luke)*
- *Letters of the Apostle Paul – Romans to Philemon (the next 13 books)*
- *Letter to the Hebrews – author uncertain*
- *Letters of James, Peter, John and Jude (the next 7 books)*
- *Revelation – a prophetic book written by the Apostle John to do with the future and proclaiming*

the Bible complete, nothing more to be added to it, the final book of the Bible

Job is considered the oldest book of the Bible, estimated to be 2000 BC, followed by the writings of Moses, approximately 1500 BC. However, the book of Genesis is assumed to be compiled by Moses but based on writings and verbal traditions from the first man, Adam, through to Abraham, Isaac, Jacob and his 12 sons, the beginning of the nation of Israel. So, the contents of Genesis clearly pre-date the life of Job, who was considered to be before, or near the time of Abraham.

Hence, the Old Testament was written, apart from Job, between 1500 BC and 400 BC, and compiled along the way. Its recognition as Canon (the authoritative compilation) is estimated between 200 BC and 100 AD. This, in essence, is the Jewish 'Bible', with the Christian Bible including this plus the New Testament.

The New Testament was all written in the first century AD, or at least by 120 AD, and most of it in the middle of the first century (35 AD to 70 AD). It was made Canon by 400 AD.

Why Christianity

Other books, called apocrypha, have been added by some parts of the Christian church (Roman Catholic and Orthodox), to both the Old and New Testaments, but these are not recognised generally by all Christianity. (More on the apocrypha in Part 4, chapter 1)

Chapter 2 Beginnings and Historical Continuity

Beginnings:

In Part 1 of this book, we were led to the conclusion that the universe, and mankind, had a beginning, and that such a beginning required an omniscient, omnipotent, pre-existent God. This conclusion arose from the scientific evidence supporting the Big Bang starting point, the lack of any plausible scientific theory to explain biogenesis, the scientific evidence refuting the theory of evolution, and the scientific, archaeological and historical agreement with the Biblical creationist account (apart from the creation events themselves which are beyond the scientific remit). So this consideration of a 'beginning' has to be the initial consideration of which faith, or what faith, must be true, because the true faith has to be consistent with the objective evidence. I can believe that the Earth is flat and worship the Sun as a deity, but this is not consistent with the objective evidence, and it is wrong (incorrect). It is not a rational choice.

So, the first evidence of the True Faith is having a rational, albeit supernatural, beginning, a coherent transition from that beginning to modern man, and a story that is 'scientifically compatible' (consistent with scientific knowledge and laws apart from explicit supernatural events). Christianity (along with Judaism and Islam) has such a beginning, and it is recorded in the first book of the Bible, Genesis.

The book of Genesis describes the beginning and the transition to modern man. It starts as follows:

> *In the beginning God created the heavens and the earth. Now the earth was formless and void, and darkness was over the surface of the deep, and the Spirit of God hovered over the waters. And God said, 'Let there be light' and there was light. God saw that the light was good, and he separated the light from the darkness.*

As discussed in Part 1 Chapter 2, this short, four sentence narrative has an amazing likeness to our modern scientific description of Big Bang to formation of Earth, which I will attempt to describe with the benefit of modern scientific understanding as follows:

> The Big Bang singularity occurred, for which the laws of Physics as we know them, did not apply, and the four fundamental forces of the universe began. It began at a seemingly infinite temperature, if temperature even applies, and through expansion and the resulting cooling, subatomic particles started to form. After just 20 minutes, neutrons and protons formed, but it was

still too hot to capture electrons and form neutral atoms. The universe was opaque to light (light was trapped, reabsorbed and unable to travel). By about 370,000 years, the universe cooled enough for neutral atoms to form, and the universe became transparent. Visible light started to be emitted from atoms relaxing to their ground state – 'Let there be light!'. And the radiation we now observe as Cosmic Microwave Background Radiation was emitted. Sometime in the 200 to 500 million year range, early generations of stars and galaxies formed, with potentially very large stars having very short lifetimes, relatively speaking, resulting in supernovae that filled the universe with all the elements we know today. It is from the stardust of these early generation stars that our present stars and planets have formed, and, in particular, our solar system.

After about 7½ billion years, our solar system formed with the sun and the planets forming at about the same time. It was dark, apart from starlight and the light emitted from the extreme volcanic activity on the surface of the Earth, and an atmosphere was forming around the Earth, from the volcanic emissions, producing a vast canopy of water vapour as well as other gases. At some point, the Sun's core became hot enough for nuclear fusion to begin and the Sun began emitting light, with the moon, if it existed at this point, reflecting that light.

Now compare that with the 4 sentence narrative in Genesis.

> *In the beginning God created the heavens and the earth.* **The Big Bang singularity.**

> *Now the earth was formless and void, and darkness was over the surface of the deep, and the Spirit of God hovered over the waters.* **The first 200 million years or so. The gases hydrogen and helium had formed and early stars were forming, our Solar System and Earth had not formed yet (formless and void). The waters may refer to gases, or to molecular water formed after the early stars' supernovae.**

> *And God said, 'Let there be light' and there was light. God saw that the light was good, and he separated the light from the darkness.* **The light emitted when the universe became transparent and/or the shining of the first stars, radiating light throughout the universe and dispelling the darkness. Still no Sun and Earth.**

Then the Genesis narrative continues with:

> *God called the light 'day' and the darkness He called 'night'. And there was evening, and there was morning – the first day.*

At this point, since there is no Sun or Earth, it begs the question what is meant by evening, morning and day. Clearly, a 24 hour Earth day doesn't apply as there is no Earth, and no Sun to produce a morning or evening on the Earth. It seems to me reasonable to read this as the completion of the first stage of God's creation plan, creation of the physical universe and setting it in motion.

The second 'day' in Genesis could be read as the formation of the Earth and the completion of the second stage. 'Day 3' is the preparation of the Earth's surface for habitation and forming the 'seeds' of the plants to come. Only in 'Day 4' does the Sun begin to radiate light, illuminating the Earth and the Moon and enabling the growth of plants, from the 'seeds' of day 3. 'Day 5' sees the **creation** of living creatures, sea life and birds, according to their kinds. Then on 'Day 6' the rest of land creatures are formed and finally, man is **created**, in God's image.

These are the 6 'days' of creation, and notice that the act of **creating** only occurred 3 times, all the rest was forming or making. The first creation was the physical universe (including plants) on day 1. The second creation, on day 5, was living creatures, which are from the dust of the physical universe, but also they have what might be called a **soul**, which required a creative act. Finally, the third creation was man on day 6, which are also from the dust of the physical universe and have a soul, but also have a **spirit**, to be in the image of God, and this required the third creative act.

As a reader, you may be challenging or disagreeing with some of the details above, or with my attempt at interpreting the Genesis account through our modern view of the universe and its origins, but that is, to some degree, missing the point. The Genesis account can be verified to be written over 2000 years ago. In fact, it is believed to be written/compiled by Moses 3500 years ago, from the writings and verbal retelling of the patriarchs before him, including Adam, Enoch, Methuselah, Noah, Eber and Abraham. As I expressed in Part 1, human intelligence has not substantially changed from Adam to now, but knowledge has, and certainly scientific understanding has. So, what could we expect for a description of the beginning of the universe and the formation of our solar system and earth from writings of 3500 years ago? Additionally, all of this was done by God prior to Adam coming into existence, so it can only come from what God revealed to Moses or those who came before him. At the time of Moses there were no telescopes, and they knew nothing of the universe, really, as compared to what we know today. So, in fact, the first chapter of Genesis is a remarkably detailed description of the origins of our universe, solar system and earth, with scientific insight, regarding sequence, that has only been gained in the last 100 or so years. Here, I would suggest, the Bible is unique in having a scientifically compatible description of the origins of the universe and our world as we know them today.

So, the first evidence of the True Faith, a rational story of our beginnings, is met in Christianity, and in Judaism, through the book of Genesis, in the Bible.

Historical Continuity:

The Christian faith is not a new religion started about 2000 years ago, but rather it is born out of Judaism, which itself stems from Abraham, the father of the Jewish nation. Once again, the source can be found in the book of Genesis, and it even traces back to the first man, Adam, providing that transition from the beginning to modern (historical) man. In Genesis chapter 5 we are given a line of descent from Adam to Noah, with details about life spans and ages at the birth of the next in line such as,

> 'When Jared had lived 162 years, he became the father of Enoch. And after he became the father of Enoch, Jared lived 800 years and had other sons and daughters. Altogether, Jared lived 962 years and then he died.'

Apart from the exceptionally long life spans, which I addressed in Part 1 Chapter 7, we see a continual line of descent outlined with details. In fact, one man, Enoch, was considered to be a prophet whose writings were preserved and are referred to in the New Testament letter, Jude. The book, or books, of Enoch with manuscripts dating back to 200 or 300 BC, were common knowledge in the time of the early Christians (first century AD), are part of the apocryphal text included in some Christian Bibles today and are universally ascribed to Enoch, the seventh from Adam. What we see here is that the 10 individuals named in this family line, from Adam to Noah, are **historical**, and show continuity from the first man, Adam, to Noah, the first man of the post-flood world.

Next came the Flood; and I feel I must digress slightly. Many people, at least in my generation (and I include myself), were brought up on a diet of Bible **stories**, with emphasis on the word, **stories**, because that is how they were presented to us, as stories, not historical events. In fact, the whole Bible was considered to be full of such stories – which ultimately led to me forsaking the

Christian faith, in my 20's, as a religion based on stories, not the truth. Now, believing the events such as the Flood to be true, does not make a person a Christian, nor does not believing them to be true preclude a Christian faith. The Christian faith is in Jesus Christ as our Saviour, Lord and God. But being presented with the events of the Bible as true to start with surely makes it easier to take the next step to believe in Jesus. The Flood was an historical event. Whether it was truly worldwide or not I will leave for another to argue, as there are times where the Bible refers to the 'world' yet clearly is talking only about the middle east regions or the Roman world. I repeat, the Flood was an historical event, and there is evidence of it found on all continents, but that is not my issue in this book, so I will digress no further.

Following the Flood, Noah and his family became the progenitors for all the races and peoples throughout the world. Genesis chapter 11 outlines the family line from Noah's son, Shem, to the father of Judaism, Christianity and Islam, Abraham, and then Abraham becomes the subject of the next 14 chapters. Once again, this family line is historical, with details along the way, and it is with Abraham that God made a binding agreement that through his descendants, God would bring reconciliation between Himself and mankind.

Then, from Genesis chapter 26 onwards, we are given the people and events of Isaac (Abraham's son) to Jacob, to Jacob's 12 sons, to the move to Egypt, and finally to the bondage of the nation of Israel in Egypt. Following this, in the book of Exodus, we are told of Moses and the exodus from Egypt. The rest of the Old Testament tells of the conquest of the promised land, the Judges of Israel followed by the Kings of Israel, the exile and return of Israel, and finally, in the apocrypha, the occupation of the Romans. This then concludes the Old Testament, leading into the New Testament and the birth of Jesus.

Essentially, the Old Testament includes an historical timeline from the first created man, Adam, right through to the Roman occupation of Palestine, just over 2000 years ago. This is what I refer to as historical continuity from the beginning. **And the Abrahamic religions (Christianity, Judaism and Islam) are the only faiths with this historical continuity,** as far as I know.

Remember, in this section of this book, I am trying to show that Christianity is the true faith, and the only true faith, and I include Atheism as a possible faith when I make this statement. **To be the truth, a faith should have a reasonably valid explanation of the beginning of our existence and some degree of historical continuity from that beginning to the present.** These two criteria are met in Christianity and Judaism, and possibly Islam,

The Rational Choice

through the book of Genesis and the rest of the Old Testament. Atheism is ruled out on these criteria as it has no valid explanation of the beginning of life (biogenesis), and its historical continuity is based on the theory of evolution which is disproved by the laws of Science as explained in Part 1 Chapter 6. Hence, the field of possible true faiths is already narrowed down to a field of three, just by these first two criteria, but there is much more to come.

Chapter 3 Purpose

Either there is an objective purpose to our existence, originating from beyond our existence and requiring a god or gods to have established that purpose, or there is no purpose apart from our subjective, self-established purpose. The true faith must either have this objective purpose or not, and it is important that we recognise, and consider what that means.

Consider Existentialism. In simple words, taken from philosophybasics.com, it "is a philosophy that emphasizes individual existence, freedom and choice. It is the view that humans define their own meaning in life, and try to make rational decisions despite existing in an irrational universe.". Therefore, an individual's purpose would be subjective and self-established. That purpose may be to live a benevolent life, or a hedonistic life, or a life dedicated to a cause (eg. combatting global warming), but whatever it is, the person's life can be objectively considered to be simply an event, maybe with effect, but with no ultimate meaning. This, on its own, doesn't mean that Existentialism could not be the true faith, but I certainly would not want it to be the true faith, as ultimately, it would mean that we are all meaningless. To quote Solomon in the book of Ecclesiastes (in the Old Testament), "Everything is meaningless." or from my favourite Kansas song, "All We Are Is Dust in the Wind.", both express the futility, and depressing perspective, of our lives without an objective purpose.

Conversely, the Christian faith has an objective purpose, derived from the God who created us. Our purpose is to know, love, and be in relationship with God, our creator. In the Bible, 1 John 4:8, it says, "God is love". In fact, the whole Bible expresses that God is love, and Jesus, as revealed in the four Gospels of the New Testament, demonstrates the same. Since He is love, we were created to be the object of His love, with the purpose of being in a love relationship with Him. The greatest commandment, as Jesus confirmed to a pharisee's questioning, is, " love the Lord your God with all your heart, mind, soul and strength". Equally, the first question-answer in Spurgeon's Catechism of the Christian faith is: "What is the chief end of man? Man's chief end is to glorify God and to enjoy Him forever.". Our purpose is to love God, glorify God and enjoy God, and largely that is accomplished through seeking Him, revering Him and obeying His commands and precepts. This is expressed in Old Testament language at the end of Ecclesiastes when Solomon declares, "here is the conclusion of the matter; Fear God and keep His commandments, for this is the whole duty of man.".

Just to stress the point for a minute, I want to reiterate that according to the Christian faith, our primary purpose is to be in a loving relationship with God. If this is the true faith, as I am endeavouring to show, consider how we spend our lives. Those who don't believe in God are completely missing the point of their existence, but even believers in God, and particularly Christians (and I include myself) still spend much of their lives seemingly oblivious to this, their very purpose in life. It is a sobering thought.

However, back to the point, what is the purpose of man in the other faiths around our world? In some cases that might be better expressed by asking what is the final goal, or objective, of these faiths. It might be to reach Heaven, to achieve Nirvana, to become an Avatar or to achieve transcendence. Whatever the case, it leads to the question of how to achieve that objective, and this leads to the topic of grace vs achievement which is discussed in Chapter 6 of this Part 2. But first I must continue with more evidence of the true faith.

Chapter 4 Key People and Supernatural Events

The next major consideration for identifying the true faith is the key people it is derived from and the supernatural events substantiating it. Anyone can start a new faith/religion, and new religions are being started all the time. But the fact that they are being 'started', and the fact that they are being derived from the minds of their originator, jointly confirm that they are false; they have no substantiation; they have no historical basis; they are made up, invented or created, and they are not the truth – regardless of whether they are believed or not. Some may question whether Christianity was 'started' following the resurrection of Jesus, but Christianity, the faith, was the fulfilment of Judaism, the original faith. So, who are the key people of Christianity, what are the supernatural events, and how do they show that Christianity is the true faith?

The Old Testament:

Prior to Abraham, Judaism and subsequent Christianity, did not exist as faiths, but their foundations did. Starting with Adam, the first, created man, there was no religion or faith. Adam was created by God and he knew God, his creator. Initially, he walked and talked with God, at least a physical form of God which many Christians refer to as a pre-incarnate form of Jesus. Even after being exiled from the Garden of Eden, Adam was still in relationship with God and communicating with God. Probably, God spoke with many of the pre-flood patriarchs; certainly he did with Enoch (evidenced by the prophecies and book(s) of Enoch), and with Noah (evidenced by the dialogue related to the Ark and the Flood). Without doubt, most of the pre-flood peoples would have lost their connection with God and started to worship other things (or beings – angels?), and possibly started their own religions, because of their corruption, their remoteness from God and their need to believe something. The knowledge of God, and channel of communication with God was preserved through the named line of descendants to Noah.

After the flood, this same knowledge of God and channel of communication with God is also passed down through the family line of Shem, one of Noah's sons, until Abraham. By the time of Abraham, there are people groups spread throughout much of the world, I would expect, and most of them have probably strayed far from the knowledge of God, therefore devising a multitude of beliefs and practices and religions, but Abraham and his family are not the only followers of God. In Genesis, chapter 14 we read of Melchizedek, king of Salem, who was a priest of God Most High, so there are other followers of God at that time. However, we are told in the

Bible that God chose Abraham to produce a nation of followers of the true faith, to carry that light, in a world of increasing darkness.

The key people at this point are Adam, Noah and Abraham, each of whom spoke with God and were given supernatural guidance, for supernatural events. For Adam it was living in the Garden of Eden, being warned of the Tree of the Knowledge of Good and Evil and being exiled from the Garden. For Noah it was being warned of the flood to come, being instructed in building the Ark, and being delivered into a new, post-flood world. Then for Abraham it was being guided to, and promised, the land of Canaan, being promised a nation of descendants and given a son, Isaac, in his old age, and being a witness, and even counsel to, the destruction of Sodom and Gomorrah with fire and brimstone from above. God's supernatural favour that was bestowed on Abraham for his preservation and prosperity, such as his stay in Egypt in Genesis chapter 12, his rescue of Lot in Genesis chapter 14, and his interaction with Abimelech in Genesis chapter 20, was also evidence of Abraham's faith in the one, **true** God.

Continuing from Abraham to Isaac to Jacob and even to Joseph, there was still no 'Jewish' faith, but rather the knowledge and faith in the one true God, and that continued to be evidenced by prosperity and preservation, even supernatural at times. For Isaac it was the supernatural guidance of Abraham's servant to find Rebecca, Isaac's wife; God's renewal of his promise to Abraham, now to Isaac; and Isaac's prosperity in the land of the Philistines and the witness of their king to Isaac, "we saw clearly that the Lord was with you". For Jacob the evidence of faith in the truth was his supernatural dream of the stairway to heaven and God speaking to him in the dream; his supernatural prosperity in the land of his relative, Laban; and his wrestling with God and renaming as Israel in Genesis chapter 32. Finally, this evidence of supernatural preservation, prosperity, guidance and communication continued with Joseph in his prophetic dreams; his preservation through deliverance into slavery and prison in Egypt; his supernatural interpretation of dreams; and his elevation to the highest rank in Egypt, second only to the Pharaoh.

The point in this is that the **evidence** of their faith (in the God of Adam, Enoch, Noah, Abraham, Isaac, Jacob (Israel) and Joseph) was documented, in detail, and this evidence was supernatural and acknowledged by their contemporaries. This was not an individual being 'enlightened' and disseminating this newly found wisdom with little or no validation apart from its appeal to our human reasoning, but rather an entire lineage of evidence, spanning over 2000 years, of detailed,

The Rational Choice

documented events and interventions demonstrating supernatural confirmation of God interacting with people. These people communicated with God, and it was confirmed supernaturally, to the witness of their contemporaries. Interestingly, there is little to suggest that these key people were even trying to spread their faith. They knew God, they communicated with God, and within their family they preserved the knowledge of and connection with the one, true God.

It is at this time that we also begin to see fragments of archaeological evidence to corroborate the more significant historical events such as the famine in Egypt during Joseph's time and the residence of the Israelites in Egypt for the next 400 years. This confirmation of what can be corroborated gives further confirmation of what cannot be corroborated due to lack of archaeological evidence apart from the scrolls and fragments themselves from which Genesis, and the rest of the Old Testament are compiled.

Then we continue, following the gradual enslavement in Egypt during the next 400 years, with Moses and the exodus from Egypt. Once again, the true God and the true faith are confirmed through supernatural events – the plagues on Egypt, the exodus of the Israelites and drowning of the Egyptian army, the preservation of the Israelite nation for 40 years in the wilderness and the manna from heaven that fed the nation for that time. Even the specific plagues that fell upon the Egyptians were targeted refutations of the false Egyptian gods and confirmed the truth of the God of the Israelites; the one true faith amidst the popular false beliefs.

After Moses came Joshua and the conquest of the land of Canaan, the promised land. Still, the true God and true faith are being confirmed through supernatural events and guidance. Starting with the supernatural crossing of the Jordan River (similar to Moses and the Red Sea crossing) and the tumbling down of the walls of Jericho, and then continuing with the supernatural defeat of the Canaanite nations, God was providing irrefutable evidence that He is the one true God and the faith of the Israelite people, as recorded by Moses, was the one true faith. This continued through the Old Testament with the Judges, Samuel, Elijah and Elisha, and the prophets (including Daniel) where God confirmed their testimony through supernatural interventions that caused pagan kings to confess, "Surely your God is the God of gods, and the Lord of kings" (Babylonian king Nebuchadnezzar) and "He is the living God...his dominion will never end" (Darius, king of the Medes and Persians).

Today, many, if not most, people hear or read these accounts in the Bible and consider them to be stories that are either fictional or exaggerated to the supernatural

The Rational Choice

through the retelling and recording, but they fail to consider the nature or detail of these writings. These are recorded as historical records with names, times, kings and kingdoms included that can, in several cases, be verified through archaeological discoveries, and no archaeological evidence refutes them. They have chronology that is consistent with historical chronology that we know of today, but that we didn't know of several hundred years ago. So it was recorded closer to the actual time of the events, when it could have been refuted if it hadn't been true. These accounts have detail, such as the instructions for the making of the wilderness tabernacle in Exodus, the fine detail of the law in Leviticus and the family lines in Numbers that would be pointless if these were stories and not real accounts. There are people who say, 'If Judaism or Christianity is the true faith, why doesn't their God prove it?', but the irony is that the entire Old Testament is a record of God continuously proving it. And by the end of the Old Testament we are left with the Jewish nation, in the relatively small area of the present day Israel, subjugated by the occupying Roman Empire, yet carrying the knowledge of the one true God and the one true faith in that God.

The New Testament:

Up to this point, God has been revealing Himself and giving evidence through supernatural demonstrations of His omniscience, omnipotence and omnipresence that He is the one true God, and that the Jews are His chosen people to carry the true faith in Him. This isn't a story, it isn't simply my belief, but it is the truth – the evidence is there in the people, the details, the chronology, the history, and the unrefuted supernatural events. God was not hiding. He was declaring Himself all along, in addition to His creation itself being evidence of Himself, God, the creator.

Now, in Jesus the Christ, God reveals Himself, in technicolour, through the Jews, to the whole world.

The first four books of the New Testament are called the Gospels of Matthew, Mark, Luke, and John. These Gospels give a detailed, first-hand, historical account of Jesus' 3-year ministry, as well as some detail of his pre-ministry life and post-resurrection appearances. The Gospels of Matthew and John are ascribed to the Matthew and John who were disciples of Jesus during his ministry, and subsequently two of his 12 apostles. That of Mark is ascribed to John Mark, a cousin of Barnabas (fellow missionary with the apostle Paul), who spent time with the apostle Peter and accompanied Barnabas and

Paul on a missionary journey, and much later was summoned to assist Paul. Finally, the Gospel of Luke is ascribed to Luke "the physician", who accompanied the apostle Paul in much of his missionary work, and likely spent time with other apostles, and possibly Jesus' mother, Mary, in researching his written account. All four writers were contemporaries, although only Matthew and John definitely spent time with Jesus during his ministry (pre-resurrection). Also, it is generally perceived that the Gospel of Mark was written first, and that the Gospels of Matthew and Luke had drawn upon that of Mark, resulting in the substantial overlap of these 3 Gospels.

These four Gospels tell us about Jesus: his birth, his ministry, his death, and his resurrection. The truth of Jesus becomes the basis for the truth of the Christian faith, which will be explored in the next chapter, "The Historical Jesus". Following the Gospels comes the book of Acts, also written by Luke "the physician", and then the letters of Paul (primarily), James, Peter, John and Jude, along with the letter to the Hebrews and the Revelation (to John the apostle). All of these subsequent books provide further evidence of the truth of the Christian faith, as will also be discussed later.

Chapter 5 The Historical Jesus

The year of Jesus birth is disputed (about 4 BC), the month of his birth is disputed (probably not December) and the year of his crucifixion is disputed (about AD 30), but his existence, as a Jewish man in Palestine at that time is not disputable (even though some may dispute it just as some dispute that the Earth is a sphere). As well as the obvious Jewish and Christian historical records of his life and influence, there are Roman historical records. Jesus' physical life cannot be disputed any more that the lives of Aristotle, Socrates, the prophet Mohammad (founder of Islam), Guru Nanak (founder of Sikhism) or Siddhartha Gautama (founder of Buddhism). And, to this day, it is doubtful that any other person in history has had a greater influence or following than Jesus of Nazareth.

According to sources such as Wikipedia, Jesus was the founder of the Christian religion, and thus many may think of Jesus in a similar vein with the other religious founders named above, but that would be a mistake. Rather than founding a new religion, Jesus was the fulfilment of the Jewish faith. *(It gets very tricky here with the use of 'religion' or 'faith'. I refer to religion as the system of practices, rules and expectations built up around the central faith, and as such, a religion can become significantly deviated from its central faith.)* The Jewish faith, beginning with God's promises to Abraham, was that a saviour would come, through Abraham's descendants, who would deliver God's people from their sins and usher them into God's everlasting kingdom. This basic tenet was repeated throughout the Old Testament, even before the birth of Abraham, and was the hope and expectation of the Jewish faith. Jesus was the fulfilment of this hope, and as such he was the fulfilment of the Jewish faith, not the founder of a new religion.

However, having fulfilled the Law and the Prophets (the hope and expectation of the Jewish faith), and having redeemed the world through his sacrifice (Jesus' death on the cross), he ushered in a new covenant, a new promise from God, which brought with it a very different code of practice, hence a new religion, but not a new faith. The Christian faith is in the God of the Jews, the God of Abraham, Isaac and Jacob. Only now, this God is more fully revealed in Jesus Christ.

So, what makes faith in Jesus unique, and uniquely true, to the exclusion of all other religions? Here is a list of the various points that I will try to illustrate to answer this question:

- Jesus is the fulfilment of over 100 prophecies declared and recorded in the previous 2000+ years
- Jesus was the fulfilment of the hope and faith of the Jews

- Jesus performed miracles
- Jesus was resurrected from the dead
- Jesus' followers performed miracles, then and now
- The testimony of John the Baptist, Jesus' followers, the High Priest, Pilate, the Apostle Paul, and Jesus himself, declared Jesus to be Lord, Saviour, God, the Christ, etc.
- The fact that Jesus wrote nothing

Fulfilment of Prophecies:

In the world of Science, new theories would be proposed and evidence would be sought to confirm these theories. Some of the strongest evidence of the truth or validity of a theory would be when the theory itself is used to make predictions and then these predictions would be tested. If the predictions proved true, then the theory would gain validity. Examples of this abound, but two famous examples are the derivation of the Periodic Table of the Elements (discoveries of predicted elements verified the periodic pattern theorised by Mendeleev) and the CMBR evidence for the Big Bang (discovery of the predicted cosmic microwave background radiation verified the Big Bang theory from which it was predicted). Equally, the fulfilment of previously recorded prophecies provides evidence supporting the validity or truthfulness of a belief. The more diverse those prophecies and their sources and origins, the stronger the evidence to support the belief.

I once had the photocopy of an article listing over 100 prophecies in the Old Testament that pointed to and were fulfilled in Jesus. Having lost, or misplaced, that copy, I googled 'old testament prophecies of Jesus' and had in the search results: 44 Prophecies Jesus Christ Fulfilled, The Top 40 Messianic Prophecies, 55 Old Testament Prophecies About Jesus, and then the winner, 351 Old Testament Prophecies Fulfilled in Jesus Christ. These prophecies begin early in Genesis with Genesis 3:15 (God's curse on the deceiving serpent in Eden) and continue right to the last verse of the last book of the Old Testament, Malachi 4:6. I would start my list with Genesis 1:15 where God says, "Let **us** make man in our image". Here God refers to his plurality, what we have come to call the Trinity, God the Father, God the Son (Jesus) and God the Holy Spirit. So, for me, this is the first reference to Jesus in the Bible, but below I am listing a small sampling (just 17 references) of these Old Testament prophecies which were fulfilled in Jesus.

> Genesis 3:15 "I (God) will put enmity between you (Serpent – Satan) and the woman (Eve), and between your offspring (seed) and hers; he will

crush your head and you will strike his heel". This is saying a man would be born, of a woman, who will, metaphorically speaking, 'stomp on the head of evil' and be bruised or hurt in the process. This foretells how Jesus' sacrificial death would be the crushing defeat of Satan, accompanied with a painful cost (strike) to Jesus.

Genesis 12:3,7 "I (God) will make you (Abraham) into a great nation...all the peoples on Earth will be blessed through you." This promise is also repeated to Isaac and then Jacob, meaning that the saviour would be born a Jew, of the nation of Israel, and even from the tribe of Judah (Genesis 49:10).

Micah 5:2 "But you, Bethlehem Ephrathah, though you are small among the clans of Judah, out of you will come for me one who will be ruler over Israel, whose origins are from of old, from ancient times." This foretells that the birth of the messiah (Jesus) would be in Bethlehem, which is the cause of King Herod's search and infant massacre in Bethlehem following the visit of the Magi. It also hints at Jesus' pre-existence, "whose origins are from of old, from ancient times".

Isaiah 7:14 "Therefore the Lord himself will give you a sign: The virgin will be with child and will give birth to a son, and (they) will call him Immanuel." The messiah (Jesus) would be born of a virgin. Also, this foretells that Jesus would be God incarnate, as he would be called Immanuel, meaning God with us.

Hosea 11:1 "out of Egypt I (God) called my son" This refers to both the bringing the nation of Israel out of bondage in Egypt, but also foretells the flight to Egypt of Joseph, Mary and Jesus (God's son) and their return to Israel.

Job 19:25 "I (Job) know that my Redeemer lives, and that in the end he will stand upon the earth" This man Job, who is considered a contemporary of Abraham, or possibly earlier, suffered great afflictions and when challenged by his accusers (that his afflictions are a result of his evil deeds – of which they could find none), responded with faith in a saviour who already existed (Jesus' pre-existence) and would one day be present physically on the earth (Jesus' incarnation).

Isaiah 40:3-5 "A voice of one calling in the desert prepare the way for the Lord ... And the glory of the Lord will be revealed, and all mankind together will see it." This foretells John the Baptist preparing the way for Jesus and proclaiming him to be the expected Messiah.

Malachi 4:5-6 "See, I will send you the prophet Elijah before that great and dreadful day of the Lord comes." This foretells John the Baptist coming, 'in the spirit of Elijah' to prepare for Jesus (the first coming), and it refers to Elijah coming again, in the future, to precede the 2nd coming of Christ.

Isaiah 53:1-12 This whole chapter is a prophecy of the saviour to come, Jesus, including: his rejection by his own people (rejected by the Jews), his taking of our infirmities (healing all illnesses), his carrying our sorrows (he bore our guilt on the cross), considered stricken by God (raised up on a wooded cross), pierced for our transgressions (for our sins, pierced by the soldier's spear), crushed for our iniquities (flogged and crucified for our sins), punishment that brought us peace was upon him (died for our sins), by his wounds we are healed (his sacrifice brought us healing and redemption), silent before his accusers (he did not defend himself in the trial before the High Priest, Herod or Pilate), placed in a rich man's tomb (placed in the tomb meant for Joseph of

Arimathea), punished and killed with criminals (placed on a cross between two criminals), despite being innocent (Pilate even stated he found no guilt in Jesus).

Psalm 22:14-18 This foretells of the crucifixion of Jesus, describing his bone dislocations, dry mouth, pierced hands and feet, naked and gaunt, and the dividing of his garments between the soldiers and casting lots for his clothing.

Psalm 69 This foretells of Jesus' rejection by his own people, his innocence and his parched throat, even given gall and vinegar for his thirst, during the crucifixion process.

Psalm 2:7 "He (God) said to me, "You are my Son"" foretelling the audible voice of God at Jesus' baptism.

Psalm 78:2-4 and Isaiah 6:9-10 Both foretell that the messiah would speak in parables.

Psalm 41:9 and Zechariah 11:12-13 Foretell that the messiah would be betrayed, and the betrayal price would be thrown into the house of the Lord to the potter. Judas threw the betrayal money into the temple and the chief priests used it to buy a potter's field.

Zechariah 12:10 "They (inhabitants of Jerusalem) would look on me, the one they have pierced." This foretells the piercing of Jesus' hands and feet at the crucifixion and his piercing by the soldier's spear.

Psalm 16:10 and Psalm 49:15 "you (God) will not abandon me to the grave, nor will you let your Holy One see decay" and "God will redeem my life from the grave". These both foretell of Jesus' resurrection from the dead.

Psalm 34:20 "he (God) protects all his bones, not one of them will be broken". This foretells that Jesus dies on the cross, so the soldiers didn't break his leg bones as they did with the criminals beside him to hasten their death.

These are just a sampling of the plethora of prophecies in the Old Testament pointing to their fulfilment in Jesus, some more general while others more specific and detailed. The whole book of Exodus can be seen as prophecy of what Jesus would be as the saviour, redeemer, deliverer, scape goat, sacrificial lamb, the Passover sacrifice, etc. I would say that the entire Old Testament points to Jesus.

Think about this. These are prophecies written between 400 and 2000 years prior to Jesus, backed up by archaeological evidence (Dead Sea Scrolls), from a range of authors, giving incredibly varied and in many cases, detailed, aspects of the messiah to come, which all came to fruition in Jesus. These prophecies were also so varied that no-one could grasp how they could all be fulfilled in one person. **This is unique!** Is there anyone else in history, much less a person upon which a faith is built, who is/was so expected and who fulfilled such numerous and varied, prophesied expectations?

I don't feel that I can emphasize this enough. The fact that all these prophecies came true is evidence that they are from the True God, that the God of all these people in history who wrote these prophecies was the True God. And the fact that Jesus was the fulfilment of all these prophecies. Doesn't this mean that He is the truth, the Messiah, the Son of God, the basis upon which the one true faith is built?

The Hope of the Jews

The hope of the Jews really starts back in Eden with the fall of man, and the proclamation by God that the seed of woman would "crush the head" of the serpent (or Satan). This meant that a man would be born who would defeat Satan, but at a cost.

Next came the promise to Abraham that his descendants would become a great nation and that "through your offspring all nations on earth will be blessed" (Gen 22:18), and that promise was re-iterated to Isaac and then Jacob. So, the Jews looked forward to one of their own being the hope of all nations.

Then the promise to Moses was "I (God) will raise up for them (the Israelites) a prophet like you (Moses) from among their brothers; I will put my words in his mouth, and he will tell them everything I command him". Hence, the Jews were looking forward to a prophet, born an Israelite, who would speak directly from God to them.

The promise to David was a blood descendent who would "build a house for my (God's) name" and whose kingdom would be established for ever. It continues, "I (God) will be his father, and he shall be my son". So, the Jews were expecting the messiah, the anointed one, to be born into David's bloodline and to usher in a kingdom that would never end. They were also expecting him to build a house for God's name, which Solomon, David's immediate son, did in the physical sense, building the first Temple, but which Jesus did in the fuller Spiritual sense through his resurrection as referred to in his words in John 2:19, "Destroy this temple, and I will raise it again in three days.", which John further explained, "But the temple he had spoken of was his body. After he was raised from the dead, his disciples recalled what he had said."

There were many other promises in the Old Testament given through the various prophets, and judges and others; all adding to the expectations and hope of the Jews. But further to these promises were the prophetic events and practices adding to the expectations and hope of the Jews such as:

- Abraham showing obedient willingness to sacrifice his son, Isaac, as a prophetic act to symbolise God's willingness to sacrifice his son.
- The sacrificial system of the temple offerings as a temporary covering of sin, or a temporary bridge of reconciliation with God, foretelling of a future blood sacrifice that would be a permanent reconciliation.
- The Passover lamb as a foretelling of the ultimate Lamb of God atonement for sin.
- The leadership and even name of Joshua (God saves) foretelling a greater Saviour to come and lead his people into the ultimate promised land.

All of these promises, prophecies, practices and events shaped the expectations and hope of the Jewish people, even though they had many, varying ideas of how these could all be fulfilled. In the end, Jesus fulfilled these expectations and hopes:

- Born a Jew / Israelite
- A blessing to all nations (salvation to all who believe in Jesus)
- An open conduit between God and man, the torn curtain at his death
- Demonstrated that he was/is the Son of God, and this was proclaimed from heaven (Mark 1:11 and 9:7), "This is my Son."
- Built a house for God's name in his resurrection and also in John 14:2, "In my father's (God's) house are many rooms …. I am going there to prepare a place for you (Jesus' disciples)".
- Born in David's bloodline and in Bethlehem (Luke 3, Matthew 1, and Luke 2:4-5 the journey to Bethlehem, the town of David, for the census around Jesus' birth)
- He came to be sacrificed, on the wooden cross, as the Lamb of God, to make atonement for the sins of all mankind, and to redeem mankind into the promised kingdom of God
- He was resurrected to rule eternally

It is also recognised that not all the hopes and expectations have been fully realised yet, as all Christians are looking forward to Jesus' Second Coming, which was promised by Jesus, and which is still to come. In this Second Coming, both the Christians' and Jews' expectations of God's kingdom, physically on earth, is to be realised.

The Jews looked for the Messiah to come, and even before there was a Jewish nation, the followers of God looked for a Redeemer to come (Job 19:25). Jesus was the looked-for Messiah and Redeemer. Where, in any other faith or religion, was there so much expectation and hope in a person to come at some time in the future, and prophesised to come by so many different sources? Jesus, the Son of Man, the Son of God, is unique! He is not just a prophet who comes to give us some new revelation from God, although he does that, but he **is** the fulfilment of prophecy; the fulfilment of the hopes and expectations of over a hundred generations of people before him.

The Miracles Jesus Performed:

At the end of the Gospel of John, the author wrote (John 20:30), "Jesus did many other miraculous signs in the presence of his disciples, which are not recorded in this book" and in (John 21:25), "Jesus did many other things as well. If every one of them were written down, I suppose that even the whole world would not have room for the books that would be written". In the four Gospels are explicit records of 37 or 38 miracles performed by Jesus. These don't include the "many healings" and the "healed them all" occurrences, along with the "many other miraculous signs" reference above. Just a few examples of Jesus' miracles are:

- Turning water into wine at the wedding
- Calming the wind and the waves on the Sea of Galilee
- Walking on water
- Multiplying the loaves and fish to feed 5000+ and to feed 4000+
- Telling Peter to catch a fish which would have the Temple tax in its mouth
- Reviving a dead girl and reviving the deceased Lazarus
- Casting out demons and restoring sanity to the insane
- Healing diseases, healing birth defects, healing impairments
- Healing long term disfigurements and conditions such as leprosy

Some of these miracles were done in small gatherings with only a few witnesses, but many of them, if not most, were done in public spaces where there were literally hundreds or thousands of witnesses. No one, from the time of Jesus until now, has rationally refuted that Jesus did these miracles. Sure, there are those who don't believe the miracles happened, but they cannot refute the miracles because there is no evidence with which to refute them, and this is because they weren't refuted at the time of Jesus, or at the time of the disciples after Jesus death and resurrection, or at the time of the writing and circulation of the Gospels. There were too many witnesses of the miracles for them to be refuted. Even Jesus' opponents, the scribes and pharisees who pressed for his execution, didn't refute the miracles but rather persecuted Him for some of the miracles being done on the Sabbath (Mark 3:1-6).

Again, faith in Jesus is unique! What other faith is based on a historical person who is documented to have performed innumerable miracles, and of such diverse variety, who claims to be the Son of God and who backs it up by doing what only God could do? I have heard individuals say, "if God exists and if He loves us, then why doesn't He prove it?" and my answer is, He did! And it is documented!

Jesus' Resurrection from the Dead:

In a very public display, paraded through the streets of Jerusalem, at a time of a major festival making the city of Jerusalem heave with visitors from throughout the middle east, Jesus was forced to walk with his cross, in a bloodied, beaten and viciously scourged state, to a place outside the city walls where he was nailed to that cross and crucified in front of the throngs of onlookers and accusers. He died on the cross, coincident with unusual darkness in the hours preceding his death and an earthquake at his final breath and the curtain in the temple tearing from top to bottom. Towards the end of the day, the legs of the criminals were broken to hasten their deaths so they could be taken down before the sabbath day, but Jesus' legs were not broken because he was already dead, and his death was further confirmed by a soldier thrusting a spear into his side, bringing a sudden flow of blood and water. It was clear, in a very public setting, that Jesus had died.

His body was prepared and placed in a tomb, with a guard posted at the tomb to ensure no disturbance or interference with the body or tomb, as well as a very large stone placed to block the only entrance to the tomb. The tomb was secured, and yet, on the third day, the stone was miraculously moved, the soldiers fainted, and Jesus left the tomb. In the ensuing 40 days, the resurrected

Jesus met with his followers repeatedly and was witnessed by over 500 people (1 Cor 15:6), many of whom were still alive, as witnesses, at the writing and reading of Paul's letter to the Corinthians. What is more is that Jesus was not in a revived body (such as Lazarus who would still die), but Jesus was in a resurrected body – which bore the wounds of the cross and yet would suddenly appear in the disciples' midst (John 20:19 and Luke 24:36-37) and equally disappear (Luke 24:31).

Jesus, and faith in Jesus, is unique! It is unlike any other faith or religion or religious leader in the world. What other religion or faith has a witness from beyond the grave who is documented over a period of 40 days and seen and interacted with by so many witnesses?

The Miracles of Jesus' Followers, from then to now:

Not only did Jesus do countless miracles, but his followers, over the past 2000 years have continued to perform miracles in His name. Notice that they perform the miracles in Jesus' name, and not their own. This in itself is quite astounding, that Christians, for the last 2000 years have been performing miracles and rather than claiming credit themselves, they have consistently attributed the miracles to Jesus. To the sceptics, these miracles will not be believed, but once again they are documented and, for the most part, not refuted. First, the miracles in the time of the apostles are documented in the book of Acts. Then we have reports and records of miracles over the following 1800 years in various writings, some reported to validate the sainthood of various Christian saints. More recently we have books written of various Christians' ministries, which are loaded with examples of healing miracles, usually witnessed by large groups of people. Examples of these would be John G Lake and Smith Wigglesworth in the late 1800s and early 1900s, and then modern, contemporary examples such as Heidi Baker (missionary to Africa) and Bill Johnson and Bethel Ministries (Reading, California). There are countless books citing countless miracles by countless Christians which can be verified today, and these miracles are attributed to Jesus.

Yes, we can ignore these miracles, we can generalise that they are false as certainly some of those reported miracles are exaggerations or even shams, or we can suggest that there are other explanations, but we can only make these choices because the miracles didn't happen right under our noses, and we are unwilling to do the research to check their validity. The evidence is overwhelming, in volume and extent, that these miracles are happening, by choice (not accidental), and in Jesus' name. This is clearly not the same for any other faith.

The Rational Choice

The Testimony of Those Present:

Jesus did not become the Son of God, the Christ, the Messiah, the Saviour, the Lamb of God or the Son of David at some time in the future, long after his departure as his reputation grew in the imaginations of his followers, but he was recognised as such by his contemporaries, both followers and opponents.

- John 1:29 "The next day John saw Jesus coming towards him and said, "Look, the Lamb of God, who takes away the sin of the world."" This was John the Baptist introducing Jesus to the Jewish nation.
- Matthew 16:16 "Simon Peter answered, "You are the Christ, the Son of the living God."". This was the response of Peter, Jesus' disciple, when asked by Jesus, "Who do you say I am?".
- Mark 3:11 "Whenever the evil spirits saw him (Jesus), they fell down before him and cried out, "You are the Son of God."" This occurred many times, and Jesus rebuked the spirits, ordering them not to tell who he was as it was important for it to progressively become evident to people through his works and words, and for the conflict with the Jewish leaders not to come to a climax too early, before the appointed time.

- Mark 10:18 ""Why do you call me good?" Jesus answered. "No-one is good – except God alone."" Here, Jesus was challenging the understanding of the questioner, to challenge him to understand what he (the questioner) was actually saying, but Jesus did not refute what was said.
- Matthew 21:9 "The crowds that went ahead of him (Jesus) and those that followed shouted, "Hosanna to the Son of David! Blessed is he who comes in the name of the Lord."" Also, John 12:13 "Blessed is the King of Israel." These are the crowds of Jews heralding the entrance of Jesus into Jerusalem, riding on a donkey.
- John 11:49 "Then one of them, named Caiaphas, who was high priest that year, spoke up, "You know nothing at all! You do not realise that it is better for you that one man die for the people than that the whole nation perish."" Caiaphas said this prophetically, not realising that he was referring to Jesus as the sacrifice, or the Lamb of God.
- John 11:25-27 "Jesus said to her, "I am the resurrection and the life. He who believes in me will live, even though he dies; and whoever lives and believes in me will never die. Do you believe this?" "Yes, Lord" she (Martha) told him, "I believe that you are the Christ, the Son of God, who was to come into the world.""

The Rational Choice

- John 4:25-26 "The woman (Samaritan woman at the well) said, "I know that Messiah is coming. When he comes, he will explain everything to us."" Then Jesus declared, "I who speak to you am he." Here Jesus confirms to the Samaritan woman that he is the Messiah who has come. Later the other Samaritans from that town confessed, "We no longer believe just because of what you (the woman) said; now we have heard for ourselves, and we know that this man really is the Saviour of the world.".
- John 20:28 "Thomas said to him (Jesus), "My Lord and my God!"" Having seen the proof of Jesus identity after the resurrection, Thomas, one of the disciples makes this confession, and Jesus confirms his belief.
- John 19:14 ""Here is your king," Pilate said to the Jews." Pilate is acknowledging that Jesus is the King of the Jews, and he goes on to write that on a sign fastened to Jesus' cross.
- Mark 15:38 "And when the centurion, who stood there in front of Jesus, heard his cry and saw how he died, he said, "Surely this man was the Son of God.""
- The beginning of John's Gospel, John 1:1-18, which I am including here, despite its length, because of its significance:

"In the beginning was the Word, and the Word was with God, and the Word was God. He was with God in the beginning. Through him all things were made; without him nothing was made that has been made. In him was life, and that life was the light of men. The light shines in the darkness, but the darkness has not understood it. There came a man who was sent from God; his name was John. He came as a witness to testify concerning that light, so that through him all men might believe. He himself was not the light; he came only as a witness to the light. The true light that gives light to every man was coming into the world. He was in the world, and though the world was made through him, the world did not recognise him. He came to that which was his own, but his own did not receive him. Yet to all who received him, to those who believed in his name, he gave the right to become children of God – children born not of natural descent, nor of human decision or a husband's will, but born of God. The Word became flesh and made his dwelling among us. We have seen his glory, the glory of the One and Only, who came from the Father, full of grace and truth. John testifies concerning him. He cries out saying, "This was he of whom I said, He who comes after me has surpassed me because he was before me." From

> *the fulness of his grace we have all received one blessing after another. For the law was given through Moses; grace and truth came through Jesus Christ. No-one has ever seen God, but God the One and Only, who is at the Father's side, has made him known."*

- And finally. we have the Apostle Paul declaring about Jesus in the Letter to the Colossians, "He is the image of the invisible God, the firstborn over all creation. For by him all things were created.... For in Christ all the fulness of the Deity lives in bodily form."

So, from all contemporaries, friend, foe or just observers, Jesus was acknowledged to be the Son of God, the Christ, the Messiah, the Saviour, the Lamb of God, the Son of David and more.

Jesus Wrote Nothing:

This seems like an odd sub-heading for this section of how faith in Jesus is unique and uniquely true, but consider this, that most religions are based on the writings of their founder (eg. Mormonism and Joseph Smith). The faith of Christians is based on what everyone else wrote about Jesus and the things he did and said (the Gospels), and what they wrote about his followers (the

Acts of the Apostles) and what was written to flesh out the underlying principles (the New Testament letters). Jesus was the greater revelation of the God of the Jews, the God of the patriarchs, the God of Adam and Eve, the God of creation. Jesus did not produce writings to describe God or a religion, but rather He was God, among us (the people of his time), to give a much greater, first-hand revelation of the God who is from the beginning. He was not a god, but the One and Only God. He did not produce reasoned ideologies to win over the hearts and minds of people, but rather, he **revealed** himself, through his teaching and his works. The Christian faith is based on who Jesus was (and is). What he taught springs out of who he was/is and guides us on how to live out that faith in Him.

Summary:

So, lets sum this up. How does a historical Jesus make Christianity uniquely true?

To begin with, Jesus' incarnation was foretold, by various sources for over 2000 years before he was born to Mary, and in great detail, not just vague impressions. Only God can know the future. Not only was his coming foretold, but as a result, Jesus was expected and hoped for by the Jews, and he fulfilled those expectations, although not in the way that the Jews of his time expected them to be fulfilled (a sacrificial death to conquer Satan and establish God's kingdom rather than a physical overthrow of the Roman occupation). Jesus' irrefutable miracles demonstrated that he was sent by God and that he had the power of God, and his resurrection from the dead demonstrated his power over death and his divinity. The miracles of Jesus' followers from then until now further demonstrate that Jesus is God and is empowering his followers to continue to do his works. The testimony of Jesus' contemporaries shows that they believed in his divinity and power as much then as we do today and that his memory has not been a growing exaggeration. And finally, the uniqueness of Jesus' sacrificial atonement on the cross, for the sins of the world, sets Christianity apart from all other religions. Christianity is unique, it is the truth and in the words of Jesus himself, "I am the way and the truth and the life. No-one comes to the Father except through me." (John 14:6)

Chapter 6 Saved by Grace (Salvation by Faith and not Works)

This topic really deserves its own chapter, not for the volume that needs to be written, but rather for its significance. Man-made religions come out of our human mentality which seems to be wired with the concept of earning or accomplishing or deserving. We feel a pride in having earned or accomplished something, and we then feel we deserve the spoils of our accomplishment. And this is the basis of virtually all religions apart from Christianity. Most religions have rules that must be kept, practices that must be done or sacrifices that must be made for salvation to be obtained. That might be as simple as 'right living' or 'being a good person', but it still is a criteria to be met. And having met the criteria, many would say that they deserved the resulting salvation, except for the problem that we never seem to be able to fully satisfy the criteria – to be perfect. Christianity is unique in that it is based on Grace and Faith rather than works or accomplishment. It can be summed up in these verses:

> John 1:12 "Yet to all who received him, to those who believed in his name, he gave the right to become children of God"

> John 3:16 "For God so loved the world that He gave His one and only son, that whoever believes in Him shall not perish but have eternal life."
>
> Romans 3:22-25 "This righteousness from God comes through faith in Jesus Christ to all who believe .... For all have sinned and fall short of the glory of God, and are justified freely by his grace through the redemption that came by Christ Jesus. God presented him as a sacrifice of atonement, through faith in his blood."

For Christianity, it is simply a trust issue. You can't earn your way to heaven, you can't deserve your way into heaven, you can't buy or barter or offer sacrifices to get into heaven. The only way to get to heaven is to trust in the blood of Jesus' sacrifice to atone for your sin and redeem you into God's family. You can only be saved by faith, and not works or accomplishments, and that makes Christianity unique.

However, this is not necessarily such a simple concept for us to understand. For most religions or faiths, it is an endless struggle, in this life, to be, and remain, 'good enough'. For many, especially the humble, they rarely see themselves as good enough because they are constantly aware of their failings, if even just in their thoughts, whereas others, especially the arrogant, will usually see themselves as good enough because they are able to ignore or disregard their failings. So, which is actually 'good enough'? For Christians this is the wrong question because no-one is 'good enough'. Rather, the criteria is believing in Jesus and thereby accepting the gift of God's grace.

So where does this debate within the Christian faith about faith vs works come from? It stems from the fact that our beliefs have consequences – they impact our attitudes and behaviour. If we believe in Jesus, that will impact our attitudes and then our behaviour in ways which will demonstrate to ourselves and others that our belief is sincere. The works (our behaviour) become evidence of our faith, and without that evidence our faith may be questioned by ourselves and others – but God sees the heart, the evidence isn't for Him. So it is the faith, belief in Jesus, that is the criteria for admission into God's kingdom, and the works, or rather the passions behind the works, that are the evidence that give us confidence in the sincerity of our faith.

In this last paragraph, I intentionally left out any mention of the Holy Spirit, for simplicity of argument, but the Holy Spirit plays an integral part in the transforming of the attitudes and behaviour of a Christian. When a person confesses their belief in Jesus, a spiritual transaction takes place. That person's citizenship transfers from the 'kingdom of this world' to the 'Kingdom of God', and as citizens of God's kingdom, His Holy Spirit comes to dwell within them, in their heart. It is God's Holy Spirit that gently and subtly changes the person's attitudes and behaviours, particularly as that person yields themselves to the Holy Spirit's influence. That indwelling Holy Spirit is the guarantor of citizenship in God's kingdom.

So how is this idea of Grace illustrated in the Bible, and how did it apply before Jesus' death and resurrection? To answer this, I first refer to the New Testament, Romans 3:22-25,28

> This righteousness from God comes through faith in Jesus Christ to all who believe. There is no difference, for all have sinned and fall short of the glory of God, and are justified freely by his grace through the redemption that came by Christ Jesus. God presented him as a sacrifice of atonement, through faith in his blood. ... For we maintain that a man is justified by faith apart from observing the law.

Next, I would refer to the criminal on the cross next to Jesus recorded in Luke 23:42-43 "Then he (the criminal) said, "Jesus, remember me when you come into your kingdom." Jesus answered him, "I tell you the truth, today you will be with me in paradise."" This criminal was saved by his belief in Jesus that he expressed during his own crucifixion. No works or deeds to earn his salvation were possible, in fact, it was his works that earned him crucifixion.

Then comes arguably the most well-known verse in the Bible, spoken by Jesus, John 3:16 "For God so loved the world that he gave his one and only Son, that whoever believes in him shall not perish but have eternal life."

So, for all people in the AD (or CE) time frame, salvation is by faith in Jesus the Christ, at least for those who have heard of Jesus. But what about those who have never heard of Jesus or those who lived prior to Jesus?

Saved by Grace before Jesus' Death:

The concept, or even proclamation from God, as to how He was to save mankind through Grace, by faith and not works, is evident from the beginning of mankind, immediately after the fall of man. After God confronts Adam and Eve about their disobedience (and in essence, their transference from His kingdom to the kingdom of this world), it says that, "The Lord God made garments of skin for Adam and his wife and clothed them." The garments were to cover or temporarily deal with the problem of their sin (manifest in their nakedness). They didn't earn or work for the garments, but God made them. Also, the cost of making the garments was the death of an animal, a blood sacrifice, which God provided. So immediately we are shown that our sin will be dealt with by a blood sacrifice that God would provide. This is the means of Grace made evident long before the coming of Jesus. Thus, from the beginning, people were saved through **their faith in God providing a blood sacrifice to atone for their sins**. This is reinforced in the next chapter of Genesis when Abel's offering (a sacrificed lamb) was acceptable, and Cain's offering (produce from his farming effort) was rejected.

Later we read about Abraham in Genesis 15:6 where "Abram believed the Lord, and he credited it to him as righteousness.". This passage is used in the New Testament, by Paul, to illustrate salvation on the basis of faith rather than works. And then, years later, Abraham believes and trusts God to the point of taking his own son up the mountain to offer him up in sacrifice, at God's instruction. On the way, he tells his son, Isaac, that "God himself will provide the lamb for the burnt offering". In the end, God withheld Abraham from sacrificing his son and did provide a ram for the burnt offering, but the reference to the requirement for a blood sacrifice, that God would provide, is crystal clear. Additionally, here is where we see that the sacrifice would be God's own son, being foretold through the near offering of Abraham's own son.

In the book of Job, we read the passage where Job says, "I know that my Redeemer lives, and that in the end he will stand upon the earth. And after my skin has been destroyed, yet in my flesh I will see God". So, Job's faith is in a Redeemer, that already exists (God) but will one day come in the flesh, and that Job himself will be resurrected to see God. Of course, Job is recognising his need to be redeemed and that God would provide that Redeemer. Once again, faith, not works.

Then we come to the tricky part of Moses and the Law. We can see several purposes for the Law given to Moses, but it was clearly not a means of achieving salvation. As Paul said in Romans 3:20, "Therefore, no-one will be declared righteous in his (God's) sight by observing the law; rather, through the law we become conscious of sin.". The Law was given to teach the Israelites about righteous attitudes and behaviour, to set the standard of righteous behaviour, to set the Israelite nation apart from the other nations they were about to displace and to maintain their distinctiveness, and even to establish rules for healthy living in terms of diet and marriage; but it was not given as a means of salvation because no one could fully meet its requirements apart from Jesus, himself. So, once again, salvation could not be earned through obedience to the law, but rather through faith in God's means of salvation.

Ultimately, it comes down to who solves the problem of how mankind is to achieve salvation, in whatever form that may be. Either **we** solve the problem, which is salvation by works or behaviour, or **God** solves the problem, which is Grace through His sacrifice, appropriated by faith. In this, Christianity is unique, and uniquely true. No-one can qualify by being good enough against the standard of a holy God, but God is able to redeem the unqualified.

Chapter 7 The Inner Witness (The Holy Spirit)

In several faiths, there is a transition or place or state of greater enlightenment that is sought, often through meditation or practised disciplines, in which the person achieves what is considered to be a greater awareness, and maybe understanding, of the spiritual state of humanity. Where that greater enlightenment comes from is another, frequently unasked, question. The answers to this may range from: the untapped power of the human mind, transcended masters, a common life force, or even revelation from the gods. However, Christianity, and Judaism before, have the unique concept of the God of all creation, in the Person of the Holy Spirit, choosing to indwell us, personally, and gently guide, teach, correct, comfort, and challenge our thinking, both conscious and unconscious, in order to transform our nature to that of God. This too is an evidence of the truth and uniqueness of Christianity, although I must concede, it is not so objectively clear.

We can see evidence of this transformation with Saul, the persecutor of the early Christians, being transformed into Paul, the eminent missionary and teacher of the growing Christian Church, as documented in Acts chapter 9 and then chapters 13 and beyond. Endless conversions and resulting transformations have taken place and been recorded from then until now. In fact, such is the case with every true Christian. One such example occurred in New York City in the 1960s that was recorded in the book, "The Cross and the Switchblade". This is an account of a Christian pastor (church leader) from upstate New York who relocated to the rough areas of New York City due to the prompting of the indwelling Holy Spirit. He started to befriend the members of the warring gangs in the city resulting in the conversion and transformation of members and key leaders of the gangs, some of whom went on to be great evangelists in their own right.

I recognise that examples of individuals converting to all religions resulting in transformed lives have taken place and that it would be very difficult to show how Christian conversions and transformations are particularly unique and led by the Holy Spirit of God. However, the evidence of the work of the Holy Spirit in the lives of Christians is there, even if it may seem subjective, and it is further proof of the truth of the Christian faith.

The Sinful Nature of Man:

Many, if not most of us, have heard the expression, "A leopard can't change its spots.". As is the case with most sayings, it bears an element of truth: we can't easily change our nature. Typically, this 'nature' would be somewhat related to our personality and behaviour, but on a broader scale, and from a Christian perspective, that nature might be called an innate sinful nature, or in my opinion, an innate self-led nature. In this context, I will be referring to the selfish nature as pursuing one's own desires and the loving nature as pursuing the desires of others or of another, and ultimately, loving God would entail pursuing the desires of God. So helping the old lady across the street can come out of either nature; selfish in doing it because it makes you feel good to do the good deed, or loving when doing it sacrificially for the old lady's sake. What this is leading to is the premise that all mankind is born with an innate selfish nature and that another evidence of the truth of Christianity is how God, through the Holy Spirit, changes that innate nature to a God loving nature. Furthermore, the recognition of the effect of the Holy Spirit on our innate nature becomes an inner witness to the Christian, of the truth of his/her faith.

I think this concept of innate sinfulness or innate selfish nature is easily misunderstood. It is less a statement about good or bad behaviour and more a statement of what the root motivation is. In the Bible this is succinctly expressed as acting out of the flesh or out of the Spirit. Out of the flesh is not only from our self-serving desires, but also our reasoning and our intentions prior to Christian faith, whereas out of the Spirit is from the guidance and will of God. An example from the Old

Testament would be when the Israelites were told, by God through Moses, to enter the promised land (the first time), and out of fear, they refused. Then, having been rebuked, they again acted on their own initiative, having now been told not to enter, and they tried to enter the land only to be defeated. In both instances they were acting contrary to God's instructions and thus out of the flesh rather than the Spirit.

To follow this point further, we need to reflect back to the reason for our existence, or even our existence itself. As was discussed in Part 1, the rational conclusion is that we were created by a god, and that this creator-god created us for a reason, or a purpose. The Judeo-Christian answer to that purpose is to be in a loving relationship with our Creator God. Understanding that our God is the very source and definition of love and goodness, trusting in Him and desiring His will over our own is the very essence of being in a loving relationship with Him. Hence the need to act out of the Spirit rather than out of the flesh. This is referred to in the New Testament book of Hebrews 11:6 when it says, "Now without faith it is impossible to please God". This statement is early in the famous chapter on faith where the writer gives several examples of faith demonstrated by those who chose to trust God and follow his guidance and direction, even when it seemed contrary to the rational or sensible or even 'good' thing to do. In

John 4:34 Jesus, who often refers to himself as the Son of Man (referring to his human nature), says, "my food is to do the will of Him who sent me", and in John 12:49, "For I did not speak of my own accord, but the Father who sent me commanded me what to say and how to say it. I know that his command leads to eternal life. So whatever I say is just what the Father has told me to say." My point in this is that the indwelling Holy Spirit is essential to a Christian, for it is through the Holy Spirit that a Christian can hear, feel, or sense the will of God.

Chapter 8 A Chronology of Our Relationship With God

In the last seven chapters, I have tried to outline how we can know that Christianity is the uniquely true faith. First, I considered how it traces right back to the beginning, of both mankind and the universe itself, and how it is consistent with ancient history, thus giving it an historical context. Next, we looked at the idea that our existence has purpose and that such purpose is derived from the Christian Faith; and after that, that there are key historical people and events that provide evidence to support the Christian Faith. Then we looked at the heart of Christianity, Jesus the Christ, and examined how his life, his miracles, his teaching, and ultimately, his sacrificial death and resurrection provided irrefutable evidence of the truth and uniqueness of the Christian Faith. We looked at the concept of salvation by Grace, which is so unique to the Christian Faith, and so philosophically necessary for the true faith, and finally we touched on the inner witness of the Holy Spirit to the truth of the Christian Gospel.

So now, I want to step back and paint a rough chronology of the relationship of man with God from the beginning until now. What happened from the first created man and woman walking and talking with the creator God, to the flood and destruction of most of the human race, to Abraham, then Moses and then to the incarnation of God in Jesus. Then finally, how it got to where it is now. This is a sort of 'big picture'.

Before the beginning was God, the only God, and a God with a triune nature, the Trinity. God's nature is love, and what is love without the beloved, so God created. God created everything that is, or was, out of his love, and to be his beloved. All of the Big Bang (and with it, time), all of the universe, all of the angels, all of the billions of years forging the celestial bodies and our Sun, Earth and Moon, all of the millions of years preparing the garden of the Earth we live on, all of the living creatures and animals, and ultimately all of mankind were created by God to be his beloved. All was created by God, and with complete foreknowledge of everything that would ever happen in time. God did not cause everything that ever happened, any more than a baseball bat manufacturer caused a Babe Ruth home run or a murder in New York city, but God foreknew. From the beginning of mankind, God was already revealing his plan of salvation in Jesus Christ – from the moment of the fall in the Garden of Eden, with the sacrifice to cover Adam and Eve with animal skins, to the test of Abraham to offer Isaac on the mountain, and the raising up of a serpent on a pole by Moses in the wilderness, God was revealing his plan. And his plan involved the redemption of mankind, and all of creation, through his sacrifice of his only begotten son, God himself in the second person of the trinity, on the Roman cross 2000 years ago. The significance, and uniqueness of this sacrifice of God himself for his beloved cannot be overstated.

> For God so loved the world that he gave his one and only Son, that whoever believes in him shall not perish but have eternal life. (John 3:16)
>
> Yet, to all who received him, to those who believed in his name, he gave the right to become children of God (John 1:12)

So, mankind was created, in perfect innocence, and dwelt with God in the Garden of Eden. Following the inevitable fall... I have to pause here and explain – why the inevitable fall? God's intent for his beloved is reciprocated love and trust. Love and trust are a choice and as such require the possibility, and inevitability, of choosing not to love or trust, at some point. The fall, by Adam and Eve in the garden, was such a choice.

Continuing on... Following the inevitable fall, mankind lived with a diminishing experience and knowledge of God, and a growing alienation from God. Adam and Eve were banished from the garden of Eden, and we read of their sons, Cain and Abel, presenting their offerings to the Lord (Genesis 4). The Lord even spoke to Cain in rebuke for the killing of his brother. So they are no longer walking and talking with the Lord in the cool of the evening, as Adam did, but they do have what appears to be face to face contact. By the way, 'the Lord' is seen by many as being a pre-incarnate form of Jesus, remembering that Jesus, the second person of the trinity, is eternal – everything was created by Him, for Him and through Him. By the end of Genesis 4 we read that by the second generation from Adam (Enosh), 'men began to call on the name of the Lord', suggesting to me that they no longer had face to face contact, and possibly little communication at all.

Genesis 5 details a lineage from Adam to Noah, a lineage of connection with God, including Enoch (the sixth generation from Adam and great grandfather of Noah) who 'walked with God' and was 'taken' away by God. During this period we also read, Genesis 6, how:

> *"the sons of God saw that the daughters of men were beautiful, and they married any of them they chose."..."The Nephilim were on the earth in those days – and also afterwards – when the sons of God went to the daughters of men and had children by them." ..."The Lord saw how great man's wickedness on the earth had become,"*

There is much speculation about this passage, but a common view is that fallen angels (from Satan's rebellion against God) were the 'sons of God' who bore children to humans forming a mixed race, the Nephilim, who were evil and were the reason for the flood – to eradicate the contaminated race. However, Noah was in an uncontaminated lineage and he still 'walked with God' resulting in his preservation, and the preservation of mankind through him.

This new start for the human race, Noah's family, were already at a diminished experience of God compared to the first start with Adam and Eve who walked and talked with God in the Garden, so it wasn't long before much of the growing population had little or no knowledge of God and they began formulating new religions. We know little of this time apart from what is recorded in Genesis 10 and 11, which includes the Tower of Babel event. Here we read that with a single language, the people of that time chose to concentrate in a city and tried to ascend to heaven. God then supernaturally multiplied (confused) their languages, inducing them to separate and scatter around the world as intended. It is clear that the connection and communication with God had greatly diminished by this point.

It is from some time after the Tower of Babel that we read the account of Job, and from this see that there are still those with a knowledge of God, and in Job's case a deep faith in a loving, redeeming God. This is also the case with

Abraham, whom God called out of his country (Ur of the Chaldeans) and away from his people, to forge a new nation of people, a chosen people, who would carry the knowledge of God and become the host for the incarnation of God in Jesus. This new nation, starting with Abraham, then Isaac, then Jacob (Israel) and then the 12 tribes of Israel, grew in the land of Egypt until the time of Moses.

Up to this time of Moses we see a clear picture of a world population losing its connection with and knowledge of the God who created everything. Other religions sprang up to suit people's tastes and imaginations, but a diminishing number were still believing in and trusting the God of all creation. Other people groups who had dispersed further from the middle east seem to have drifted further in their connection and knowledge of God, often defaulting to more animistic forms of religion. Now, with the nation of Israel formed, God raises up Moses to be his mouthpiece to the nation, to train a people in the knowledge of Him, and of righteousness and justice, and of faith and trust.

So God gave, through Moses to this Israelite nation, the Law, a set of rules, principles, ordinances, practices and punishments aimed at training them in righteous living and setting them apart from the nations and practices around them in order to prepare them, as a nation, to host the saviour to come. Where personal connection with God was disappearing, the Law became a fixed reference, an objective source for gaining knowledge of and connection with God, and a guide for maintaining that connection as a nation. Over the next 800 years, through the period of the Judges and then the Kings of Israel, the nation had its ups and downs (mostly downs) in maintaining its connection with, and knowledge of God, but through prophets God chose to speak directly to the nation, and the occasional 'rediscovery' of the book of the Law, the nation and the knowledge of God was preserved. Then came the exile or 70 year captivity.

The nation of Israel had departed so far from following the Law or seeking God, and had turned so much towards the religious practices and worship of false, man-made religions, that God let the nation be conquered, by the Assyrians and then the Babylonians, and the people exiled. This broke the downward spiral and led to a revived passion and earnest pursuit of God by those who led the return to Jerusalem 70 years later. First, they rebuilt the temple in Jerusalem and then, over the next 100 or so years, they re-established the religious practices ordained by the Law. They returned as a people more determined to know and obey God, and over the next 400 years they established the religious system of Judaism. This then became the setting, in time, place and spiritual awareness, for the most monumental event since the creation of the universe – **the incarnation of the Son of God** - the coming of Jesus.

God became man. He walked and talked with man and woman once more, but this time He offered a sacrifice that didn't just cover sin (like the skins in the garden of Eden or the animal sacrifices on the alter), but it cancelled sin and provided a path of uncorruptible connection with God, the Father. When Jesus' sacrifice on the cross was finished, the curtain in the temple, separating God's holiest dwelling from mankind, was torn in two. Access to God was restored, and the path was through Jesus.

> *"I (Jesus) am the way, the truth, and the life; no one comes to the Father except through me."* John 14:6

After Jesus resurrection from the dead, and before he was raised up to heaven, He imparted His Holy Spirit (the third person of the Trinity) to his disciples (John 20:22), and they were later 'filled' with the Holy Spirit at Pentecost (Acts 2). These Spirit filled followers of Jesus led others to faith in Him and the indwelling of the Holy Spirit, but the Jewish leaders, who rejected Jesus out of pride, arrogance and jealousy, started a persecution of the followers of Jesus that resulted in the dispersal of those followers throughout the Roman empire, and beyond. These followers of Jesus Christ started to be called 'Christians' and so began the 'Christian Church'. Essentially, the Christian faith is the faith of Abraham, Issac and Jacob, fulfilled in Jesus Christ, and then going forward from that point.

The last, nearly 2000 years, has been a process of the growth of the Kingdom of Heaven – God's Kingdom on Earth. Jesus came preaching, "Behold, the Kingdom of Heaven is at hand.", because He was the gate to the Kingdom. The Kingdom is entered through faith in Jesus, and the last 2 millennia have seen the growth of this Kingdom from a small group of disciples to hundreds of millions worldwide.

This leads to the next two parts of this book, 'Being a Christian' and 'Which Christian Church', which will hopefully make more sense of what it means to be a Christian and how the religion of Christianity has developed since the early followers of Jesus.

The Rational Choice

Part 3: To Be a Christian

The Rational Choice

Part 3 Introduction:

In Part 1 of this book, I presented the evidence and rationale as to why belief in an omnipotent God is the most rational choice. In Part 2, I presented the evidence and rationale as to why belief in Jesus the Christ is the most rational choice, above all other religious and 'non-religious' beliefs. In Parts 3 and 4, I seek to explain what it means to be a Christian and how to comprehend, manage, and navigate the religion of Christianity. First, however, I need to start with becoming a Christian – making that step if you haven't already, and I want to make it clear that becoming a Christian is not joining a church or a club. Becoming a Christian is simply about belief and confession. That's it; no hoops to jump through. But having said that, it is the most important decision you will ever make in your life, and not just in this physical realm, but in the Spiritual realm as well (to be discussed in chapter 5 of this Part 3).

I repeat, choosing to believe in Jesus is the most important decision you will ever make in your life. Think about it. If the Christian faith is the truth (which is what I have been trying to argue through the first half of this book), then communion with God, through Jesus, is the reason we came into existence, and choosing to follow that reason or reject that reason is of prime importance. Jesus came preaching, "repent, for the kingdom of heaven is at hand", and choosing to believe in Jesus (with the consequential repentance) is the entrance to the kingdom of heaven, God's kingdom. Furthermore, it is pretty clear throughout the Bible that we only have this life to make that choice, no reincarnation. Jesus reinforced that there is a resurrection to new life, or final judgement, but that final destination depends on this life's choice.

Chapter 1 How to Become a Christian?

This is the shortest and simplest chapter in the book.

To become a Christian, you must believe in Jesus, the Son of God; that He gave His life for all our sins, that He rose from the dead to eternal life and that He has the authority and power to give eternal life to every person who believes in Him. Then you must declare this, sincerely, out loud, to God and to another person. That is it!

And your first Bible verse to remember is John 3:16, 'For God so loved the world that He gave His one and only Son (Jesus), that whoever believes in Him shall not perish, but have eternal life.' And the next one is John 1:12, 'Yet to all who received Him (Jesus), to those who believed in His name, He gave the right to become children of God.' And finally, Romans 10:9, 'That if you confess with your mouth, "Jesus is Lord," and believe in your heart that God raised Him from the dead, you will be saved.' Notice here, that to 'believe in Jesus' involves choosing to follow Him, thereby choosing Him to be your Lord as well as Saviour.

So, in becoming a Christian, you become a child of God, your sins are atoned for and forgiven, and salvation, the kingdom of heaven, is yours – simply by believing and declaring. No one can earn it, you can only receive it. This salvation is by the grace of God. So, let's look at this idea of Grace.

Chapter 2 The Principle of Grace

Grace is not what we typically would describe as fair. Jesus illustrated this in his parables, two of which I mention here:

1. The parable of the workers called to the vineyard (Matthew 20: 1-16)
2. The parable of the prodigal son (Luke 15: 11-32)

And these parables not only illustrate the 'unfairness' of Grace, but also they guide us into the attitude of Grace and the intended attitude of a Christian.

In the first parable, the workers are called at different times throughout the day to work in the vineyard for the rest of the day, hence some of them work many hours and some only a few. Yet, at the end of the day they were all paid the same amount. Obviously the first workers were disgruntled to find that the latter workers, who worked only a short time, were paid as much as they who had worked all day, despite it being a fair wage for their full day's work.

In the second parable, one son claims his inheritance early, squanders it carelessly (and in so doing dishonours his father) and then returns home in complete shame, and remorse, seeking only the station of a lowly servant in his father's house. The father is overjoyed at the return of his son and throws a banquet, while the other son feels the unfairness of the celebration and honour shown to his underserving brother and not to him.

Both parables have the idea of grace, or unmerited favour or blessing, extended to the undeserving, and the deserving getting what they deserved, but no more, resulting in their grievance. And clearly, in both parables, the aggrieved are rebuked for feeling aggrieved. Why couldn't they feel joy for the blessing or grace extended to the others? But both parables illustrate the nature of God's attitude toward us, his undeserving children – receiving unmerited grace.

With the workers, we can see the equal blessing to all, regardless of some being more deserving and some less deserving, suggesting how God loves us all and blesses us regardless of how much we may deserve or not deserve blessing; He causes the sun and rain to fall on the righteous and unrighteous equally. But we can also see how God, like the landowner, is sovereign (and also omniscient) and thus has the right and the knowledge to give blessing where he chooses; and who are we to challenge this or feel aggrieved by His choices? Furthermore, we are to have an attitude like God of loving one another and being glad and joyful for the blessing or good fortune of others, rather than one of resentfulness or envy.

Many quote GRACE as an acronym – God's Riches At Christ's Expense. It is unmerited blessing. It is not fair, it is loving. I repeat, it is not fair, it is **loving.** Each and every one of us is saved solely by God's grace, in Jesus Christ. That is Christianity.

Chapter 3 What does 'Being a Christian' mean?

In a nutshell, being a Christian means believing in the Lord Jesus Christ. Unpacking that sentence has been the subject of countless books and sermons, and it has been expressed, practised, re-defined, and packaged in the plethora of divisions and denominations of the Christian church. The core beliefs of 'believing' have been expressed in various creeds such as the Apostles' Creed, the Nicene Creed, the Athanasian Creed and many others. If you check Wikipedia for a list of Christian creeds, it is astonishing, the number of creeds, catechisms, confessions, declarations, articles, statements, etc. that have been produced in the different Christian churches to try to clarify what is meant by Christian Belief. One would hope that in all of these writings, the core principles or essence of each is the same, however that could be debated to some extent. Nevertheless, I am going to attempt to lay down some basic principles underlying all, or nearly all, of these writings, which I then intend to elaborate on. Being a Christian involves believing these underlying principles, and allowing that belief to inform and shape our attitudes and behaviour.

Underlying Principles

1. God is eternal and the source of our existence.
2. God is good and all He has done, is doing and ever will do is good. Likewise, God is love, and always acts out of His nature of love.
3. Mankind is fallen, displaced in nature from that of God, and needing redemption (restoration to God's kingdom) and sanctification (process of being made Christ-like).
4. Jesus, the Christ, is God incarnate (God embodied in human form). God is triune: Father, Son (Jesus) and Holy Spirit (or Holy Ghost).
5. Jesus' death on the cross was an atoning sacrifice for our sins.
6. Jesus was resurrected from the dead.
7. Salvation is through Christ alone.

Below is a brief list of statements in the Bible exemplifying these principles:

- In the beginning, God created the heavens and the earth (Genesis 1: 1)
- In the beginning was the word, and the word was with God and the word was God... The Word became flesh and made His dwelling among us... grace and truth came through Jesus Christ (John 1: 1-17)

- God is love (1 John 4:8)
- For all have sinned and fall short of the glory of God (Romans 3: 23)
- Just as the result of one trespass (sin of Adam) was condemnation for all men, so also the result of one act of righteousness (Jesus' sacrifice) was justification that brings life for all men (Romans 5: 18)
- For the creation was subjected to frustration (Romans 8: 20)
- For in Him (Jesus Christ) all the fullness of Deity (God) dwells in bodily form (Colossians 2: 9)
- I will send Him (the Holy Spirit) to you.... He will guide you into all truth. (John 16: 7, 13)
- Make disciples of all nations, baptising them in the name of the Father and the Son and the Holy Spirit (Matthew 28: 19)
- Of first importance; that Christ died for our sins (1 Corinthians 15:3)
- For God so loved the world that He gave his only begotten son, that whosoever believes in Him shall not perish but shall have eternal life (John 3:16)
- We know that since Christ was raised from the dead, He cannot die again. (Romans 6: 9)

- Jesus answered, "I am the way and the truth and the life. No one comes to the Father except through me." (John 14: 6)

So let's have a brief look at each of these basic principles:

Principle 1: God is eternal and the source of our existence

God, and God alone, in the fullness of the Trinity, is pre-existent. God is outside of time, not bound by time or space, as He created time and space and everything that is or ever has been. So, God, as the creator, is the One who endows us with purpose and meaning. Since God caused me to exist, my life belongs to Him, and my purpose and meaning in this life are derived from Him. This is a fundamental belief of Christianity, and although we don't always think, act, or behave in a manner consistent with this, it is still true.

Principle 2: God is good and all He has done, is doing and ever will do is good. Likewise, God is love and always acts out of His nature of love.

This is a principle that we Christians (and other faiths as well) keep repeating over and over to remind ourselves and hopefully embed in our psyche this fundamental truth. When we seem to have unanswered prayer, when suffering comes to us or our loved ones, when we hear of horrific world events or read of events in the Old Testament, we often find ourselves questioning this principle. However, as the pre-existent creator, God is the very definition of good. We don't define what is good, but rather God does, and our sense of goodness is derived out of that which God imprinted in us. Equally, God's essential nature is what we call love, because that is what He calls love. It is the core nature of God from which He acts, especially in His acts of creation, and thus He has imprinted in us the capacity to be like Him, to love and to act from a nature of love. However, love, by its very definition, has to be an act of freewill – it has to be a choice, and this is what goes to the heart of Judaeo-Christian belief. Freewill is the underlying reason for the fall of mankind, our corruption, and our need for salvation.

Principle 3: Mankind is fallen, displaced in nature from that of God and needing redemption and sanctification

Mankind was created with God's nature (in His image) and with the freewill to be able to deviate from that nature. Inevitably, the deviation occurred, and mankind was corrupted, in nature, from that of God. A transition took place where the will of Man became elevated over the will of God and this affected the very core of our nature so that it was inherited by all the human race, and through mankind to all of creation (Romans 8:20-21).

With God's will being loving goodness, any will of ours that is contrary to God's is therefore contrary to loving goodness, and therefore sin. Hence, elevating our will over God's is sin and corruption, and cannot be in union with God. So, atonement is needed for our sin (eg. a life), in order to be redeemed back into union with God, and sanctification is needed to restore our nature to that of God's.

Principles 4: Jesus, the Christ, is God incarnate; the Trinity

This is the principle that Jesus is God, he is not a created being. This is foundational to the Christian Gospel, to His power, to His worth, to His Grace. In the incarnation, God takes the form and nature of pure, sinless man, in order to identify with mankind, to provide a worthy atonement for the sins of all mankind and to establish an eternal king for all mankind. Salvation is through Jesus Christ, and He alone, because He is God. It is foretold in the Old Testament and woven throughout the New Testament. This is inherent to the concept of the Trinity, the principle that God, the one God, is expressed in three persons, Father, Son, and Holy Spirit. In today's technological terms, we might say that Jesus is God's interface with mankind, established by the Father and whom we now experience through the Holy Spirit (this is a metaphor, not a statement of doctrine).

The Rational Choice

Principle 5: Jesus' sacrifice on the cross

Mankind was categorically alienated from God because of our corruption, generally referred to as our sinfulness; the unholy set apart from the holy. In giving His life on the cross, Jesus gave the just and sufficient price of atonement for the sins of all mankind, as decreed by God in His creation. It is a sort of balance – sin must be offset by the sacrifice of life. In the first sin in the Garden of Eden, life was sacrificed to provide the skins to clothe Adam and Eve. It was a temporary, ultimately insufficient sacrifice or atonement, which later was further exemplified in the system of animal sacrifice required under the Mosaic Law. A permanent, just and sufficient atonement for all the sins of mankind, past – present – and future, was needed, and thus provided by God in the sacrifice of Jesus on the cross.

Principle 6: Jesus was resurrected from the dead

Jesus, having atoned for our sins with His sacrificial death, then took up His human life again, in a new, resurrected form. He could do this because He was without sin (so the atonement was not for himself). Since He was uncorrupted, death had no authority over Him, and because He was God, in His resurrection, Jesus opened the gate for the resurrection of all mankind. He atoned for the sins of all mankind, but not all mankind will accept the redemption provided, so not all mankind will be resurrected to eternal life with Him.

Principle 7: Salvation through Christ alone

Restoration with God can only come through God's redeeming sacrifice of Jesus' death on the cross. Nothing else is sufficient atonement or of redeeming efficacy. This was declared by Christ in his own words when He said, "No one comes to the Father except through me." Jesus the Christ is the only entrance to the presence and kingdom of God. When He died on the cross, the curtain to the holiest place in the Temple, the symbolic presence of God, was torn open. Jesus opened the way to God. He **is** the way to God.

These principles become a filter through which we, as Christians, view and interpret ourselves and the world around us. If we truly believe these principles, then our attitudes and behaviours are inevitably being changed to become more consistent with these principles. This is the process of Sanctification and is the work of the Holy Spirit in us in collaboration with our freewill.

(A sort of footnote at this point is that it almost appears that this 'filter' of Christian principles looks a lot like 'our truth'. All Christians have been led to Christ through the loving kindness of God in opening our eyes and hearts to the truth of the Gospel, but not all Christians have had the information and apologetics to defend our faith to be The Truth, the objective truth, rather than just 'our truth' based on our subjective experience. Nevertheless, Parts 1 and 2 of this book were written to show that the Christian faith is The Truth, and therefore more than just 'our truth'. That is why these principles **should** become our filter, as they are based on objective truth.)

One last word, however, on the practical reality of walking out this process of sanctification. It is collaborative, meaning we must also engage in the process and make choices in the process. To this end, we try to establish disciplines, practices, habits, and routines to encourage this process of sanctification to proceed, and it is out of this endeavour that the 'religion' of Christianity evolved. In this next chapter, I will try to expand on the distinction between the Faith of Christianity and the Religion of Christianity.

Chapter 4 Faith and Religion

Faith

'Faith is being sure of what we hope for and certain of what we do not see' (Hebrews 11:1). Faith is more than just belief: it has an element of certainty without tangible proof, and certainty such that we live and behave in a manner consistent with the object of our faith being true.

When I look across the room and see a wall there, it doesn't involve faith to believe in the wall; I can see it and touch it. However, I behave in a manner consistent with the wall's presence in that I don't try to walk through it, I aim for the doorway. Similarly, if I had faith in the presence of an invisible wall, I would not try to walk through it, but rather I would aim for the invisible doorway in the wall.

So also, faith in God is not just acquiescence to the existence of God, but it involves a certainty in God that is reflected in our behaviour and lifestyle. Clearly, the nature and attributes of that God which we have faith in will determine the behaviour that flows out of that faith. Hence, if our faith is in a harsh, strict God of the written Law, lacking grace and compassion, then our behaviour becomes very legalistic and more radicalised and extremist, executing God's judgement on those who don't submit to the literal law (as we see it). But if our faith is in Jesus Christ, and a God of love, grace, compassion, and forgiveness, then we exhibit love, grace, compassion, and forgiveness in our lives.

The point is that our faith is the mindset that informs our behaviour. Everyone has a faith, whether conscious or subconscious, whether well thought out and understood or just existentially adopted and not understood at all; we all have a faith, and that faith informs our attitudes and behaviour. Additionally, that faith can change as a result of life experiences or the exposure to new information. The whole reason for writing this book is to present new information that may change, refine, or consolidate the faith of its readers.

Religion

Religion, on the other hand, is the system of practices and expectations that we consciously formulate, both individually and corporately, and that we adopt as a way to live out our faith. If faith is the adopted reality, religion is the system of rules we formulate for that reality. For Christianity, faith is the belief in Jesus Christ as God, our Saviour, as revealed in the Bible and as experienced through the indwelling of the Holy Spirit, and religion is the system of practices formulated within the different Christian churches, and individually, which are adhered to as an expression of that faith. Christian religion includes all the sacraments (baptism, communion/mass, marriage, etc), all the church buildings and services, all the symbols, icons and shrines, the canonization of saints, all the 'should do's' (go to church, read the Bible, pray, act kindly and generously, etc.) and shouldn't do's, and the annual celebrations (Christmas, Easter, etc.), and so much more.

Religion is a necessary evil – and I mean that as a form of expression rather than a literal statement. Religion, largely, preserves the knowledge, the history, and the understanding upon which our faith is based and preserved from generation to generation. Without religion, how would I have been made aware of Jesus Christ and grown to know and love Him, and thus acquire the Christian faith? But at the same time, it is Christian religion, and particularly the 'should and shouldn't do's', that ensnare followers back into a legalistic 'have to be good enough' mentality that is the antithesis to God's Grace in Jesus Christ, and thus a corruption of the Christian faith. This was expressed by Jesus towards the religious leaders of the Jews when He said to the teachers of the law and the pharisees, 'You travel over land and sea to win a single convert, and when he becomes one, you make him twice as much a son of hell as you are.'. The religious leaders He was speaking to were winning converts to their legalistic **religion** of Judaism rather than to faith in the God of Abraham, Isaac, and Jacob.

The Rational Choice

The crusades of the Middle Ages and the indulgences of the Roman Catholic Church at that same time were prime examples of the **religion** of Christianity being used in complete contradiction to true Christian faith. And yet, throughout that period there were Christian movements in Europe whose religion was largely consistent with the Christian faith such as the Anabaptists, the Waldensians, the Albigenses and others. And certainly, within the Roman Catholic church were individuals and groups whose Christian religion may have been under the umbrella of the Roman Catholic Church but not subscribing to the excesses and politicism of the Roman church, and these groups' sub-religions may well have been largely consistent with the Christian faith.

Going back to the necessity of the religion of Christianity, we can also see how the religious practices are indispensable for introducing, teaching, encouraging, refining, and sustaining our Christian faith. This is why 'going to church' is such an important element of a Christian's life – not to satisfy the should do's, but to give and receive the teaching, encouraging, refining, and sustaining of our faith. This is why it says in Hebrews 10:25 that we should not neglect meeting together. Without the meeting together in church or house groups, we become more susceptible to our faith being dissipated by other concerns and demands and pressures of daily life. These tend to erode our passion and devotion to our faith, and eventually even erode our underlying beliefs – which Jesus referred to in the parable of the Sower (seed that fell among thorns). So therefore, whilst I am very critical of religion and the religiosity of the Christian Church, I am also very thankful for the Christian Church and recognise its importance to all Christians.

This will lead into the final section of this book, Which Christian Church, in which I will examine the history of the Christian Church and discuss the pros and cons, pitfalls, excesses, and benefits of the plethora of Christian churches. But first, three more important concepts need to be addressed; the spiritual realm, 'not a bed of roses', and baptism.

Chapter 5 The Spiritual Realm

As alluded to at the start of this section of the book (Part 3), there is both a physical realm and a spiritual realm. The physical realm is commonly referred to as the universe, from the Big Bang to the present, and is bound by time. We are conceived and born into the physical realm. However, God is outside of the physical realm, just as He is outside of time. God created the physical realm, and in doing so, created time. Hence, there is a higher realm, God's realm, which Christians refer to as the Spiritual realm. The physical realm is temporal, bound by time, but the Spiritual realm is eternal, it is not bound by time.

In John 3:3, Jesus states, "I tell you the truth, no-one can see the kingdom of God unless he is born again.". He goes on to explain, "no-one can enter the kingdom of God unless he is born of water and the Spirit. Flesh gives birth to flesh, but the Spirit gives birth to spirit.". The flesh is in the physical realm, while the Spirit is in the Spiritual realm. When a person turns their belief to Jesus and confesses Him as their Lord, that person is born again, born into the Spiritual realm, and gains eternal life because the Spiritual realm is eternal. Jesus goes on to say, "Just as Moses lifted up the snake in the desert, so the Son of Man must be lifted up" (pointing towards His future crucifixion), "that everyone who believes in Him may have eternal life. For God so loved the world that He gave His one and only Son, that whoever believes in Him shall not perish but have eternal life.". So, 'born again' is to be born spiritually.

Hence, being a Christian doesn't just mean following Jesus, but it also means being spiritually alive, being a child of God, belonging to the kingdom of God and having access to the Father, Son, and Holy Spirit. Becoming a Christian is truly a new birth: all true Christians are born again.

Chapter 6 Not a Bed of Roses

Becoming a Christian is usually a joyful experience, but it is also commonly accompanied with pain, conflict, or persecution. It is not the 'bed of roses' that some evangelists make it sound like, and I thought this was important to include, albeit briefly. In Luke 14:25-33 Jesus explains that following Him comes with a cost, stating in verse 27, "whoever does not carry their cross and follow me cannot be my disciple".

Most new believers experience joy for one or more of the following reasons:

- The enlightenment of knowing the truth and perceiving the world and their lives in this new perspective that gives meaning to their lives and context to everything that is.
- The recognition that they are loved by their Father, God; that they are known deeply and accepted and valued and cherished.
- The release from shame and guilt from the past through acceptance and forgiveness in Christ Jesus.
- The acceptance into the family of believers, the church
- Freedom from the judgement and demands of this world

- The experience of being overwhelmed by the presence and love of God

That joy is real, and it is sustaining, and it is enduring. It doesn't fade, although it may seem less intense with time as it permeates deeper. But, becoming a Christian does not mean that life will flow smoothly from that point onwards. In fact, the converse may often be the case, and that is the point of this small chapter.

Jesus said that to follow Him, you must take up your cross daily – your cross, representing sacrifice and death to self. At the end of the Beatitudes, He said "Blessed are you when people insult you, persecute you and falsely say all kinds of evil against you because of me." (Matthew 5:11). It is repeatedly stated in the New Testament that followers of Christ will face persecution. In 1 Peter 5:8-9 it says, 'Your enemy, the Devil, prowls around like a roaring lion looking for someone to devour. Resist him, standing firm in the faith, because you know that your brothers throughout the world are undergoing the same kind of sufferings.' And many other verses express similar warnings, the Christian life is not smooth sailing.

In the book of Acts we can read of the various persecutions faced by some of the early Christians, not to mention later persecutions under Roman emperors of the first to third centuries. But trouble in a Christian's life is not due to persecutions, necessarily. Christians are not immune from natural disasters, family conflicts, job conflicts, or any other form of everyday distress. It is a misconception to think that God will shield Christians from trouble, but it is a reassurance to realise that God will use trouble in a Christian's life for their good, as it says in Romans 8:28, 'And we know that in all things God works for the good of those who love him'. God is always with us, especially in times of trouble. Quoting Psalm 23:4, "even though I walk through the valley of the shadow of death, I will fear no evil, **for you are with me**". We are never alone.

When each of us becomes a Christian, we each become a child in God's family, adopted into the family of God. We are held, precious, in the hands of God. And that is our joy, despite what gets thrown at us in this world. Our perspective on life and purpose changes, which may mean we lose some relationships, as well as gain others, and the losing can be painful, but God is with us. Essentially, Christians are not protected from pain and suffering, in fact, we may be more prone to it as a result of persecution or the loss of relationships, but we are never separated from the love of God in Christ Jesus!

Chapter 7 What about Baptism?

There are certain actions in a Christian community which may be referred to as Sacraments and Rites, meaning that they have important spiritual significance as well as physical or emotional significance. The two most recognised of these sacraments (or rites) among most Christian churches are Baptism and Communion/Eucharist. The sacrament (or rite) of Baptism is what I want to address briefly here, as it can be a confusing issue, particularly to new Christians.

The meaning of Baptism can be expressed in a multitude of ways with equally as many nuances, but generally it involves passing through water in making a transition to a new life. The Old Testament of the Bible is full of examples of the principle of baptism:

> Noah and family passing through the flood waters, leaving behind the evil pre-flood world and emerging into the new, purified post-flood world.

> The nation of Israel passing through the Red Sea, leaving behind the life of bondage to the pagan Egyptian kingdom, and emerging into a God-led freedom heading for the promised land.

> The stubborn and rebellious Israelite nation passing through the Jordan River, leaving behind

their failings and disobedience in the wilderness, and emerging into the promised land with renewed conviction to follow God, their Lord.

In Judaism, baptism was largely associated with purification, which also included the conversion of an individual to Judaism. Then, out of this tradition came John the Baptist, preaching and administering a baptism of repentance (turning away from one's previous sinful ways) for the forgiveness of sin. John's role was to prepare the way for, and proclaim the arrival of, the Messiah (the Saviour, the Son of David, the Anointed One, etc.), and preparing the way involved confronting the Jews with their sinfulness and inviting them to repent and be baptised as a demonstration of that repentance, for purification.

Then Jesus, being without sin and having no need for repentance or purification (as acknowledged by John), came to John the Baptist to be baptised, saying "Let it be so now; it is proper for us to do this to fulfil all righteousness." Matthew 3:15. Initially, this seems unnecessary to us, as it did to John, but Jesus regularly referred to himself as the 'Son of Man', identifying himself with mankind and therefore demonstrating the way, for all mankind, into the kingdom of heaven, which begins with repentance. John's baptism represented this repentance through the dying to the former sinful inclinations (going under the water) and being raised up to new righteous inclinations (coming up out of the water). So, Jesus set the example, for all to follow, but that's not all.

When Jesus rose up out of the water in his baptism, the Holy Spirit descended upon him, like a dove, and a voice from heaven proclaimed, "This is my Son, whom I love; with him I am well pleased." God not only endorsed the act or practice of baptism, but He confirmed its Spiritual significance. John had previously stated that he was sent to baptise with water, but the saviour to follow would baptise with the Holy Spirit. Following Jesus' baptism, John testified that he saw the Holy Spirit descend upon Jesus like a dove, confirming that Jesus "is the Son of God" who would baptise with the Holy Spirit. Thus the baptism of Jesus linked the physical act of water baptism with the Spiritual act of baptism with the Holy Spirit. Hence there are two baptisms, a physical public demonstration and a spiritual, personal transaction, and they are both ordained by God.

Notice that Jesus did not begin baptising with the Holy Spirit until after his death (atonement for our sins) and resurrection (establishing himself as the gateway to heaven – "No-one comes to the Father except through me."). This is stated in John 4:2 where it says that, 'in fact, it was not Jesus who baptised, but his disciples', prior to His death and resurrection.

Following Jesus' resurrection, he breathed on his disciples and said, "receive the Holy Spirit". Then, prior to his ascension into heaven, he instructed his disciples to "go and make disciples of all nations, baptising them in the name of the Father and of the Son and of the Holy Spirit" (commonly referred to as the Great Commission). Finally, at Pentecost (50 days after Passover or 49 days after Jesus' resurrection), the disciples (now apostles) were 'filled with the Holy Spirit'. So, how do we bring this altogether into a coherent understanding of Christian baptism and of its place and practice in the Christian Church?

Water Baptism

Both John the Baptist and then Jesus preached "Repent, for the kingdom of heaven is near.". So, first, baptism is a public declaration of repentance from a former sinfulness. But following Jesus' resurrection, He told his apostles to baptise in the name of the Father, the Son, and the Holy Spirit, giving an extra dimension to it. This means that going under the water represents death to self (the former life before faith in Jesus), and coming up out of the water represents being raised to new life in the kingdom of God, new life in Jesus' resurrection. Hence water baptism, in the name of the Father, the Son, and the Holy Spirit, represents a public demonstration of a spiritual transaction of laying down one's own life to be lifted up into new life in Christ.

So who should be baptised and when and how? These questions can be hotly contested between Christian denominations, but I will give my thoughts and opinions as a starting point:

- Baptism in water demonstrates a person's choice to repent of their former sinfulness, their former subjection to self, and their former religion of works (earning their own salvation), to a life of righteousness, subjection to Christ, and faith in His atonement. It is a choice, an act of will, and therefore is undertaken by a believer in Christ, generally a newer believer, but not always. It is the 'right' thing to do, as Jesus demonstrated (Matthew 3:15), but not essential for salvation as evidenced by the thief on the cross next to Jesus (Luke 23:42-43), and by the gentile believers with Cornelius who had received the Holy Spirit as proof of their faith and salvation prior to being subsequently baptised in water in the name of Jesus (Acts 10:44-48).
- Believers should make every effort to be baptised in water in Jesus' name (or the name of the Father, the Son, and the Holy Spirit). Not only did Jesus set the example, but it was his command to his

apostles (the Great Commission, Matthew 28:19-20), and we read throughout the book of Acts how new believers were always baptised in water in Jesus' name.

- Believers should be baptised in water in Jesus' name even if they had previously been baptised as an infant (not their choice) or baptised for repentance but not in Jesus' name. Baptism as an infant does not represent their choice, hence the importance of being baptised as a believer, and baptism for repentance alone does not include the fulness of Christian baptism as evidenced in Acts 19:3-5 when Paul re-baptised the believers in Ephesus who had previously been baptised in John's baptism.
- Water baptism is preferably done by immersion (whole body dunked under water) because this is the example of Jesus and the predominant example given in Acts, and because this better represents the death to self (going under the water) and being raised in Christ (coming up out of the water). However, there is no explicit rule or command given in the Bible requiring baptism to involve full immersion, so I see it as preferable but not essential – especially when full immersion is not available or accessible.

Receiving the Holy Spirit and Being Filled with the Holy Spirit

Just as water baptism is seen as a contentious issue between the Christian denominations, the receiving and filling with the Holy Spirit is contentious as well, and more so. The two primary passages demonstrating these events are:

- John 20:19-22 When Jesus first appeared to His disciples after His resurrection, He breathed on them and said, "Receive the Holy Spirit.". This is the fulfilment of what Jesus said in John 14:16-17, "I will ask the Father, and He will give you another advocate to help you and be with you forever – the Spirit of truth. ...for He lives with you and will be in you.", and in John 16:7, "it is for your good that I am going away. Unless I go away, the Advocate will not come to you; but if I go, I will send him to you.". So Jesus had to go away (die) and be resurrected before He could send the Advocate (Holy Spirit), but in John 20, Jesus is now resurrected and so He sends the Holy Spirit, and the disciples receive the Holy Spirit.
- Acts 2:1-4 'When the day of Pentecost came, they (the apostles) were all together in one place. Suddenly a sound like the blowing of a violent wind came from heaven and filled the whole house

where they were sitting. They saw what seemed to be tongues of fire that separated and came to rest on each of them. All of them were filled with the Holy Spirit and began to speak in other tongues as the Spirit enabled them.' This was the filling with the Holy Spirit. This is repeated with many believers throughout the book of Acts, as in the example with the Ephesus believers in Acts 19:6 'When Paul placed his hands on them, the Holy Spirit came on them and they spoke in tongues and prophesied.'

Again, there are many different views on these, and many other passages in the New Testament where the Holy Spirit is spoken of, but I will again give my opinion as a starting point:

- Receiving the Holy Spirit: All believers receive the Holy Spirit when they first believe in Jesus and confess their belief, as Jesus promised. This is the Advocate, who will be in them, always. It is not an experience that we necessarily feel or consciously recognise, but rather a spiritual transaction that becomes evident in our thoughts and inclinations going forward (I am not saying that it can't be felt or 'experienced'). The Holy Spirit is always in us, but we can be more or less attentive to His inner voice. This then is what took place in the John 20 passage above when Jesus breathed on His disciples and they received the Holy Spirit. There were no particular signs or wonders, but the transaction took place and the Holy Spirit dwelt in them from that point forward.

- To be Filled with the Holy Spirit: This is a special experience that Christians may have where they consciously recognise an overwhelming presence of the Holy Spirit in them, frequently accompanied with spontaneous speaking in tongues and praising God, as seen throughout the book of Acts. It is generally a temporal experience, but it may be repeated many times throughout a believer's life, and it may bring with it an empowerment for a Spirit-led calling or for demonstrations of the miraculous (healings, words of knowledge, prophecy, supernatural ability, etc.). Sometimes a person may experience this at the same time as their water baptism; sometimes it is experienced by the 'laying on of hands' (a hand on the shoulder or head) by another believer; sometimes it is experienced in group revivals; sometimes it is experienced when a person is alone. It is to be desired by all believers, but only Jesus can perform it, according to His will.
- Baptism in the Holy Spirit: Jesus pours out His Holy Spirit upon all Christians, as we have all

received the Holy Spirit. So we can say that we have all been 'baptised' in the Holy Spirit. However, the more Pentecostal churches apply the expression 'Baptism in the Holy Spirit' to the additional 'filling with the Holy Spirit' as opposed to the general receiving of the Holy Spirit. Hence the more Pentecostal churches actively encourage believers to seek the baptism in the Holy Spirit from the Lord Jesus, referring to this additional filling.

Joy Unspeakable by Martyn Lloyd-Jones was a book I found very helpful in trying to understand this subject amid the many perspectives found in churches.

This whole topic about baptism leads nicely into the final section of this book, Which Christian Church, because it illustrates the complexity of how interpretation, nuance, and even culture will influence how a system of practices is built up around a principle from the Bible. The Bible is the reference manual, but how it is put into practice is the role of the Christian Churches.

The Rational Choice

Part 4: Which Christian Church

The Rational Choice

Chapter 1 Beginnings and the Bible

Where It Started

Church history is fascinating, but I wouldn't call it very good advertising for the Christian faith. This will become evident in the second chapter of this section, but first we need to look at the beginning of the Church and especially at the Bible, the foundational, God inspired writings underlying and defining the Christian faith.

The **religion** of Christianity all started in the first century, quite obviously, after the resurrection and ascension of Jesus, the Son of God. There were 11 disciples, renamed apostles, one freshly appointed apostle (to make it 12 again), and a very large host of faithful followers – along with a powerful horde of persecutors (the leaders of the Jews). Hence, without the physical Jesus present, it fell to the 12 apostles, under the guidance of God's Holy Spirit, to lead the 'church' of Christians. Straight away this introduced a challenge – who was to steer and preside over this new religion? Although the Holy Spirit was initially poured out upon the 11 disciples, Holy Spirit was also subsequently poured out on believers everywhere, so all Christians had (and still have) the inner guidance of the Holy Spirit. Hence all believers could receive revelation and guidance directly from God; it did not have to come down from church leadership. However, as that guidance can be very subtle and intuitive, the 'hearing' and understanding by the believer is highly variable and subjective, meaning that its reliability is questionable, which brings us back to the Apostles and eventually, the Bible.

So, it started with the 12 apostles having authority over matters of faith within the Christian church, but it wasn't long before a former persecutor turned believer, Saul who was renamed Paul, came along with new revelation (or divine insight), 'Gentile believers are not required to be circumcised', which challenged the Apostolic leadership. The apostles, particularly Peter, eventually came around to endorse this new teaching as well as to endorse Paul as an apostle of Christ. And so the Church grew, albeit with heresies and false teachings springing up in all directions, but a central group of revered men of proven faith were looked to for authority in matters of Christian faith and doctrine. In a relatively short time, a body of writings started to come together and be circulated throughout the rapidly spreading Church which included **the four Gospels** (Matthew – attributed to the apostle Matthew; Mark – attributed to John Mark in the book of Acts; Luke – attributed to Luke the physician accompanying the apostle Paul; and John – attributed to John the apostle, exiled to the island of Patmos), **the book of Acts** (same author as the Gospel of Luke), **the letters** of **Paul the apostle**, **the letter to the Hebrews** (author uncertain), some **further letters by Peter, John, James, and Jude**, and finally **the book of Revelations** written by John the apostle. This body of writings eventually became endorsed, arguably within the first century AD, as the core canon of the New Testament of the Bible, and this body of writings, along with the Old Testament, became the authoritative manual of the Christian Faith, the Bible.

The Bible

As this is the authoritative manual of the Christian Faith, we need to look at where it came from and how it came into being. The simple answer is that God inspired men (or women?) to write histories, prophecies, songs, laments, revelations, accounts, wise sayings, guidance, rules, and instructions, over a period of ± 1100 years for the Old Testament and less than 70 years for the New Testament. God inspired others to collate those sacred writings into a canon (a compilation of writings that all relevant spiritual leaders concurred on them being sacred writings from God). This happened primarily by 400 BCE for the Old Testament (the Hebrew Bible) and largely by 100 CE for the New Testament.

(Note: I am trying to use BCE and CE for consistency sake, but they effectively mean the same as BC and AD respectively.)

The Old Testament, which can also be called the Hebrew Bible, begins with Genesis (including the Creation) and finishes with the writings of Malachi the prophet. The first 5 books (Genesis, Exodus, Leviticus, Numbers, Deuteronomy) – also called the Pentateuch - are ascribed to Moses, but clearly the content of Genesis would have had to come from earlier writings, oral history, or divine inspiration as it preceded Moses' birth. Next are the historical books of Joshua, Judges, Ruth, 1&2 Samuel, 1&2 Kings, 1&2 Chronicles, Ezra, Nehemiah, and Esther (generally written by the named author or contemporary scribes), which roughly span from 1400 BC to 400 BC. Then come the so-called poetic books of Job, Psalms, Proverbs, Ecclesiastes, and Song of Songs. The latter three are generally ascribed to King Solomon; Job is ascribed to Job (in a time frame similar to Abraham in Genesis – so one of the oldest books); and Psalms written by David, Moses and Asaph primarily. Finally come the books of the prophets Isaiah through to Malachi, written by the named prophet or their scribes, and spanning the time from roughly 840 BCE to 400 BCE.

These writings were regarded as sacred writings, inspired by God, and meticulously preserved and copied, and eventually compiled into the agreed upon canon of the Old Testament. The authors were devoted servants of God, authenticated by miracles, fulfilled prophecy, and the witness of their contemporaries. The literal validity of the Old Testament is further confirmed by the regularity with which it is quoted in the New Testament (by Jesus, Paul and others), and by its very literal fulfilment in the New Testament, such as the crucifixion of Jesus so vividly described in Isaiah 53, Psalm 22, Psalm 34 and more. Regarding the preservation and accuracy of these writings, because they were considered sacred texts, the scribes that copied them did so under a mantle of divine responsibility, allowing nothing short of perfection. Hence, when older manuscripts are discovered, such as the Dead Sea Scrolls, they have been compared with manuscripts several hundred years more recent and found to be almost flawlessly reproduced, unlike any other writings of antiquity.

Then came the New Testament, written between 33 CE and 95 CE, which contains the 4 Gospels, Acts, 13 letters of Paul, 8 letters of James, Peter, John, Jude, and another, and the final book of Revelation. This too has many cross-referencing validations (one author validating or quoting another author), as well as the validation of contemporaries. For instance, the miracles of Jesus were performed publicly, often in front of thousands (eg. The feeding of the 5000), so that they could have been, and would have been, easily refuted had they not been true. This is also true of Jesus' resurrection with over 400 witnesses to his resurrected appearances. Finally, just like the Old Testament, these accounts, letters, and final book of prophecy were ultimately compiled, with Divine guidance, into the canon of the New Testament.

Thus, the Christian Bible was completed, with the Old Testament covering everything before Jesus' incarnation, and the New Testament covering Jesus, his death and resurrection, and the start of the Christian Church. The Old Testament covered the dealings of God with men under the Covenant of the Law (the criteria of Self-Righteousness) while the New Testament covered the dealings of God with men under the Covenant of Grace (the criteria of Righteousness in Christ). The Old Testament teaches us what sin is, the severity of sin, the consequences of sin, and the bondage of sin. The New Testament teaches us the unfathomable gift of Christ's atonement (Jesus' sacrifice on the cross atoning for our sins), the incomprehensible promise of His resurrection for us (that we can be resurrected to eternal life in Christ), and the indescribable freedom available in Christ (no longer in bondage to sin and death). Many Christians prefer to disregard the Old Testament, but it is the foundation upon which the New Testament is built, just as the law and the prophets set the foundation from which Jesus is the fulfilment (Matthew 5:17).

Therefore, the Bible is the Divinely inspired Word of God in written form. Its authors were inspired, its compilation was inspired, and its interpretation and use must be inspired. Think about it, it only makes sense. If God wants us to know Him, in truth rather than our imagination, he needed to provide us with a truthful, God inspired, objective source of truth and knowledge. The reasonings and teachings of men are corrupted and subject to bias and error. The Bible is God's gift to mankind as a reference of truth to which all other doctrines, teachings, philosophies, and reasonings of man must be measured against. Hence the cry of the Reformation, "Sola Scriptura!". Church history is probably the most obvious, irrefutable evidence of the need for the objective text of the Bible, as we will see later on.

So what is the inerrancy of the Bible about?

Many, if not most, Christians would say that the Bible is the inerrant Word of God, meaning that it is a direct, flawless, communication from God to man. There are various books available presenting the arguments and evidence for this belief in its inerrancy. Much of the evidence would fall into these categories:

- Historical – the historical information in the Bible has consistently been shown to be correct,

despite challenges requiring new archaeological evidence to vindicate the Biblical account (eg. Hittite ethnic group)
- Prophetical – prophecies recorded and then fulfilled hundreds of years later (eg. King Cyrus for return from exile prophecy in Daniel; prophecies of Jesus birth, death, miracles, deeds, in great detail throughout the Old Testament)
- Internal Consistency – Despite having about 40 different authors spanning over a thousand years, the Bible (Old and New Testaments) is internally consistent, having no actual contradictions, although many apparent contradictions. (eg. Genealogy of Jesus in Matthew is paternal while in Luke, maternal, hence not contradicting)
- Cross Referencing – Various parts of the Bible are referred to in other parts of the Bible, validating their 'inspired' status. (eg. Jesus frequently quoting Old Testament; Peter's 2nd letter referring to Paul's letters)

However, there can be much debate over the details of what exactly is 'inerrant'. If we look at the levels of construction of the actual Bible that I read, my list would be as follows:

> The original message of God to the author

The original writing of the text (original manuscripts)
The copying of those manuscripts, and recopying
The compilation into the official canon
The translation from copied manuscripts to a new language
The revised translations within a language
The copying and printing of the translated Bible

For some, the inerrancy would be in the original writing of the text (in the original language of Aramaic, Hebrew or Greek), and the copying and translating, and compiling were still inspired or guided by God, but not inerrant. For others it may be just the original message from God, but errors or flaws already creep in with the first writing. Still others may hold to God maintaining the inerrancy right up to the printing of the translated Bible. I knew one Pastor who held that the King James Version was the only inerrant **English** translation of the Bible.

The point is that the Bible is God's message to us. Even if the current translation that I read is not perfect, it is very close, and God is using it to communicate to me as I read it. The Bible is God's revelation of Himself, and His relationship with man, in a written, essentially unchangeable narrative. It allows us to know God, first hand (providing we can read the text), rather than through the filter and bias of others. It is second only to having lived and walked with Jesus, as the disciples did, and possibly even better as we, reading the Bible, are not distracted by His physical appearance. God created us to be loved by Him and to love Him, and He provided the Bible to enable us to know Him, in order to love Him. Yes, Him, and not the god of someone's imagination.

As an example of what I mean by knowing God truly, I will give an opinion that many might consider highly controversial, possibly offensive. Some would suggest that the Christian God, the Jewish God and the Moslem God are the same. I would disagree, but to explain, I will use an analogy of an actor. One person knows the actor personally as a friend. The second knows him through the media (interviews, public appearances, tabloid articles, etc.) and the third person knows him through the role he played in a movie. Is the actor they know the same? Clearly, the 3rd person knows a false image based on an unreal characterisation (a fictional role in a movie). The 2nd person knows a real, but only sketchy, and possibly distorted idea of the actor (a public image), whereas the 1st person knows the actor the best, having the fullest revelation of his character through first-hand experience. Similarly, the God that is known to a Moslem is based on the Quran, which was written in the 7th century, over 900 years after the Old Testament was completed, and containing several similar but altered passages to those of the Old Testament. Hence, I would say this is not a true revelation from God and that it presents a false image of God. The Jewish God is based on the Old Testament, so it is a true revelation, but lacks the fuller, more intimate revelation of Jesus and the New Testament. Hence, it is only sketchy, and distorted by the legalism of the law-based Old Testament. Finally, the Christian view of God, based on Old Testament and New Testament revelation, is the best, most complete revelation of His true nature, informed by His incarnate presence among mankind. So, yes, all three faiths are referring to the same creator God, but with different degrees of accuracy, familiarity, and validity.

The texts of a faith are the objective standards or points of reference by which all religious doctrines can be measured against and corroborated or refuted. They are the objective standard for each faith, but that doesn't make them true. That is why the writers of the Bible were authenticated by God through miracles and prophetic utterances confirmed true by their contemporaries and future generations. What other faiths, apart from Judaism and Christianity, have the writers of their sacred texts been validated in such a supernatural way? God has provided us with His word, in the Bible, and validated it beyond refuting, because He wants us to know Him, in order to love Him.

Which Christian Church

What about the apocrypha?

The apocrypha are widely circulated religious writings, thought to have been written roughly between 200 BC and 400 CE, which have held varying status within Christian churches. While some of the apocryphal books are considered to be canonical by the Roman Catholic church, and by the Eastern Orthodox church, none of them are considered canonical by the Protestant churches. Generally speaking, and certainly among Protestants, they are considered useful writings of men, but not the inerrant word of God, and thus not a basis for doctrines of the faith.

Additionally, there are other writings of early Christians that were widely circulated, which are deemed New Testament apocrypha, but they are not recognised as canonical by Roman Catholic, Eastern Orthodox or Protestant churches.

What about translations of the Bible?

The arguments put forward about the modern English Bible being unreliable as it is a translation, sometimes of a translation, of texts that have been copied and recopied over hundreds of years, are simply not valid. To begin with, the copying and recopying of the early manuscripts was done as a sacred duty, and thus near to perfection. This has been verified through the impeccable consistency between recent manuscripts and older manuscripts, sometimes several hundred years apart. Then the idea of translations, sometimes of multiple translations, is also an exaggerated issue. Most, if not all, of the modern English translations of the Bible, have been translated from the original language manuscripts (Greek, Hebrew or Aramaic) or the Latin Vulgate (Latin). It is not like the game of Chinese whispers, where the final version is very different from the original, however being translations, word choice and sentence structure can vary. This is why Christians often consult two or more different versions of the Bible (in their language) to gain a fuller understanding of the meaning or application of a verse or text.

In the 1980s, when I became a Christian, there seemed to be just a few commonly used versions of the Bible, as follows (this is not a complete list):

- King James Bible or Authorised Version (1611) - revised and replaced the original Tyndale English translation
- Revised Version (1880s) - updated and improved version of the KJB using additional archaeological discoveries (older manuscripts), and from this, the New American Standard version (1901) based primarily on the Revised Version

- Revised Standard Version (1952-1977) – still basically the American Standard version with 'Lord' instead of 'Jehovah' and pronoun variations, plus the apocrypha was added as Deuterocanonical books to produce the Catholic RSV and the Eastern Orthodox RSV
- New International Version (1978) – largely a translation by Protestant evangelicals, from earliest manuscripts, aimed at accuracy and readability
- Good News Bible or Good News Translation or Today's English Version (1966) – translated by the American Bible Society, largely for a more readable version for people with English as a second language, includes sketched drawings
- The Living Bible (1971) – a paraphrase version (not a translation) intended to communicate the meaning of a passage, sometimes by expanding the text, and not a literal translation; also it is one man's interpretation (Kenneth N. Taylor)

Since the turn of the century (2000 CE) the number of versions has seemed to increase dramatically, both translation and paraphrase versions, with The Message (2002 by Eugene Peterson) becoming a hugely popular paraphrase version aimed at using modern English to make it readable and relevant.

But in the end, all the translations and paraphrase versions are still anchored in the original message from God to the original authors of the Bible; and we have this message, accurately translated, and maybe paraphrased, into English for us to read for ourselves, not through another person's filter (which has not always been the case). And God, by His Holy Spirit, helps impart understanding to us as we read it.

Chapter 2 The History of the Church

Church History and the need for the Bible

There is a Bible in most rooms in my house. In the USA, there is a Bible in most hotel rooms throughout the country. With such abundance, we readily lose sight of the incredible value of the Bible. The cover and paper are near worthless, but the message from God that it carries is beyond price.

Beginning with Moses, these sacred writings were preserved in the hands of a very few – those who were literate. They were read from time to time to the people, and the people listened to every word, because their only access to this message from God was through the reading by those few who could read. In the Old Testament, Moses proclaimed that the Book of the Law (essentially the Pentateuch) was to be read out to the gathered nation of Israelites every seven years. Clearly this practice fell away and from time to time the Book of the Law would be rediscovered, read out to the people, and the people would repent and recommit to the Lord (2 Kings 22, Nehemiah 8 and 9). But throughout the Old Testament, the people had very little access to God's written word. By the time of Jesus, every town had its synagogue and parts of the scrolls of the Law and Prophets would be read out every sabbath day in these synagogues, so the people had much more access.

Then, following the resurrection of Jesus, the writing of the Gospels took place, and letters were written, and these would be widely circulated and read out in gatherings on a regular basis so that the people could hear the word of the Lord, the message from God, and they could come to know God and worship Him. And these writings became the lifeblood of the church, communicating the knowledge of God, from people to people and generation to generation until the late 4th century and the politicisation of the church as it became the state religion of the Roman empire. Then, the Bible increasingly became the property and tool of the state church, to be used, through their filter, to control the people (crusades, indulgences, inquisitions, persecutions of so-called heretical churches, etc.), and only the elite, educated few, had access to God's word (appropriately known as the dark ages). And so began the messy, and often shameful, history of the Christian church. Following will be a very brief summary of this history, but as we look at it, we can see the absolute necessity of the Bible as an objective reference to recalibrate the doctrines of the faith as men start to distort these doctrines and promote a religion that veers further and further from the teachings of Jesus and the doctrines of the New Testament.

From 300 AD to the Present

It is not my intent to present a detailed history of the Christian church, but I wish to give a summary of this history, to set a foundation for discussing the present state of the church and a recommendation for navigation through the complicated and confusing choices to be made in choosing which church to settle into.

70 AD to 300 AD:

> Peter, the apostle, appears to have become an unofficial leader of the fledgling church beginning after the ascension of Jesus into heaven. We say this because:
>
> - The angel told the women who came to the empty tomb to go tell His disciples **and Peter** that He is risen; Peter and John were first to go to the empty tomb; Peter was told by Jesus to 'feed my sheep'
> - Peter delivered the recorded sermon when they were filled with the Holy Spirit at Pentecost

- Peter and John were brought before the Sanhedrin following their healing, in Jesus' name, of the crippled beggar
- An angel told Cornelius, a gentile, to summon Peter to his gathering, leading to the gentiles receiving the filling with the Holy Spirit, and Peter explained this to the rest of the apostles
- Peter's address at the council in Jerusalem to discuss circumcision of gentiles was recorded

Peter certainly appears to be a leader among the apostles, but at no point was he designated to be the leader. The verse where Jesus renames Simon to Peter and says 'upon this rock, I will build my church' is often misrepresented to suggest Peter is the rock. In fact, Jesus is the rock, the cornerstone, upon which He would build His church, which is why Jesus said it in response to Peter's confession of Him as the Christ, the Son of the living God (Matthew 16: 16-19). Read also Matthew 21: 33-43 and 1 Peter 2: 4-8.

However, under Jesus are many leaders of the church. Initially these were the 12 apostles, and then the Apostle Paul, followed by various bishops who were appointed by the apostles as the church grew and as the apostles died or were killed. These bishops were to maintain the purity of the faith, the truth of the faith, the integrity of the faith, the doctrines of the faith, the preservation of the faith and the growth of the faith, but equally, as Jesus made perfectly clear, they were to be servants of the church, not rulers of the church.

Immediately, even during the Apostles' lifetimes, the church was dispersed by the Judaic persecution (starting in Jerusalem) and the Roman persecutions. This meant that in a very short time, there was no central leadership of the church, but rather that the leadership was dispersed and delegated. This opened the door somewhat for heresies and false doctrines to spring up, which they did, but two principal factors maintained the truth and purity of the faith – The Biblical Canon and Jesus. I have discussed how the Bible, even this newly formed canon of the New Testament, became an objective reference for maintaining the Truth and purity of the faith, but also, it is Jesus, who said, "I will build My church", and so He divinely maintains and builds his church despite our human deviances, of which there are many. In fact, we read about a few of these deviations in the 'letters to the churches' in chapters 2 and 3 of the book of Revelation (last book of the Bible). The named list includes false apostles, the Nicolaitans, teaching of Balaam, false prophetess Jezebel and the lukewarm faith of the Laodiceans, and Jesus even states how He is sorting them out.

So, from roughly 35AD (the resurrection and ascension of Jesus) to about 312AD (the official conversion of the Roman emperor Constantine), the church was dispersed and growing, without clear central leadership. Some argue that Constantine's conversion was for political expediency, giving some indication of the proliferation of the church at that time, but regardless, his conversion made Christianity the official religion of the Roman empire and entangled church leadership with political power, the start of the State Church.

300AD to 800AD

With Christianity now approved throughout the Roman empire, this led to a diluted church having those who became Christian for expediency along with those who were Christian by faith. There was a growing distinction between 'clergy' and 'laity', a growing centralisation of leadership with councils and synods, a developing hierarchy within the

Bishops, and a developing institution of a 'priesthood' as an intermediary between common people and God. Also, various practices grew in prominence and became institutionalised such as the use of holy water, the burning of incense (brought forward from the Old Testament temple), monasticism, veneration of images and martyrs and 'saints' and Mary, baptismal sprinkling, celibacy of priests, and doctrines such as transubstantiation (literal turning of bread and wine into the body and blood of Christ Jesus) which happened in conjunction with the transition from the Lord's supper to a Latin 'mass'. With the flourishing of the Christian church under state approval, an institutional organisation developed with leadership and functional roles within the church becoming vocations, and therefore attracting people into those roles not only for reasons of faith, but also for reasons of greed, ambition, power or just simply livelihood.

Additionally, during this period, the Papacy developed. In the third and fourth century, there was already a struggle for power between leading bishops in the major centres. By the sixth century this was predominantly between Rome and Constantinople, leading to the patriarch of

Constantinople adopting the title of 'Universal Bishop' in 588AD. By 606AD the emperor of Rome conferred the title onto the patriarch of Rome, Boniface III, thus beginning the office of the Pope.

However, don't forget that, despite this very public and widely recorded history of the official church, Jesus Christ was continuing to build His church in the hearts and minds of people throughout the known world. The emerging practices, doctrines and even beliefs of the official church were not necessarily those of the local churches, although their impact would be felt one way or another.

900AD to 1500AD

By the 9th century, the struggle for power had reached a point where the head of the church in Rome and the head of the church in Constantinople excommunicated each other. This conflict continued for another century or two until in 1054AD the final, official, division between the two church bodies took place with another mutual excommunication, the Great Schism, leading to the separate Roman Catholic Church and the Eastern Orthodox Church.

This period was a very dark period, particularly for the official Roman Catholic Church. The Crusades against the Moslems occurred during this period, the Inquisitions began during this time, scriptural authority was suppressed under church authority, the official practice of Indulgences commenced, the sacking of Constantinople (a Christian centre) and the pogroms of Jews in Europe occurred, and the papacy went through a period of disrepute. The Roman Church sought to control the lives of the people under its reach, and horrific brutality was practiced under the authority of the church. Doctrines such as the Immaculate Conception of Mary were formulated and all attempts to reform or refute the excesses of the church were brutally suppressed. Some of these attempts were the Albigenses and the Waldensians in the late 12th century, and reformers such as John Wycliffe and John Huss in the late 14th century and early 15th century.

Again, despite the widely recognised history of this period, Jesus Christ continued to build His church, and the cry of Sola Scriptura arose to refocus the doctrines of men on the truth.

1500AD to present (The Reformation and Protestant Church)

> This is a fascinating area for study, particularly the many individuals instrumental in bringing about the Reformation throughout Europe. The ideas of the Reformation did not start in the 1500s, or even in the 1300s, but rather the Reformation was a movement to depart from the divergences of the Roman Catholic and Eastern Orthodox Church doctrines and practices, and to return to the doctrines and teachings of the Bible – Sola Scriptura! In fact it was a sort of 'reset' after over a thousand years of church corruption.

The Bible, and particularly the Latin Bible was formulated as early as the late 4th and early 5th century. From its earliest formulation, it lacked accessibility for the common person and was only accessible to the educated. This meant that the multitudes were led, in their understanding of the faith, by the understanding and interpretation of a small minority, which narrowed further to a very tiny minority as a hierarchy formed within the church. This created power and with power came corruption. By the 1500s, William Tyndale is famously quoted as saying he sought to 'cause a boy that driveth the plough to know more scripture than the clergy of the day', referring to the fact that much of the clergy were even unable to access the Bible due to being uneducated. Additionally, prior to the printing press of the mid-1400s, only hand written copies of the Bible existed, and this further limited accessibility. So, for the previous 1000 years, a very few at the higher levels of the corrupted Church hierarchy dictated the doctrines of the faith to the multitudes, and brutally suppressed any expression of dissent such as the Albigenses and the Waldensians.

Then in the late 1300s and into the 1400s a foothold was gained with John Wycliffe criticising the practices and beliefs of the Roman Church and (with associates) translating most of the Bible into a Middle English (before being martyred). Also, John Huss was speaking out boldly in Bohemia against the teachings and human traditions of the Roman Catholic Church; and Jerome Savonarola, in Italy, was criticising the Papal authority and the corruption of the clergy. These footholds led to firm traction with the 95 Theses of Martin Luther sent to the Archbishop of Mainz on 31 October, 1517, and posted on the door of the church in Wittenberg. Along with this was his (Martin Luther's) translation of the Bible into German. The Reformation was under way!

Further acceleration came with William Tyndale translating most of the Bible into modern English (or more modern at least), Ulrich Zwingli preaching the authority of the scriptures over erroneous church doctrines and practices, and John Calvin's extensive writings and teachings on scriptural doctrine and reformation of the church. With these translations into the languages of the people and the distribution made possible by the printing press, the Bible was now in the hands of the people to read for themselves what God had inspired and caused the writers of the books of the Bible to record, for us to be better able to KNOW GOD.

The Protestant Church was born, or should we say, churches. Thus began an ever-increasing diversity of churches called denominations. There are over a dozen major denominations starting with Baptist, Lutheran, Presbyterian, Methodist, Anglican / Episcopalian, Reformed or United Reformed, Quakers, Salvation Army, Pentecostal and Assemblies of God, etc.. Then there are the movements, practices or attitudes that cut across the denominations such as Evangelicalism,

Pentecostal and Charismatic Movements and others. And there are many more minor denominations, but the variation between denominations, and even churches, is generally down to the various permutations of a few basic **structures** such as organisational hierarchy, baptism, spiritual gifts, liturgy, worship and doctrinal conservatism.

Then there are the fringe churches which are sometimes called Christian churches but deviate to various degrees from the core beliefs of basic Christianity. Examples of these would be the Jehovah's Witnesses, Christian Scientists, and Mormonism.

- Jehovah's Witnesses – They do not believe in the Trinity and deny the physical resurrection of Jesus. They believe that Jesus was created by God, with all else created through Jesus, by God's power. They believe the Holy Spirit is God's applied power rather than a person.
- Christian Scientists – They do not believe in the Trinity, but rather that Jesus was a man and that Christ is the divine idea, and that there is no person of the Holy Spirit. They hold their book, "Science and Health" to be

on equal authority to the Bible, and they believe in spiritual healing and discourage the use of medicine or medical assistance/intervention.
- Mormonism – They hold the Book of Mormon, Doctrine and Covenants, and Pearl of Great Price to be of equal, if not greater, authority to the Bible. They deny the Trinity, believe that God is married, hold that Jesus was simply first born of God with all mankind following, deny salvation by faith alone, believe in eternal marriage and in human deification.

Chapter 3 The Churches of Today

First, let's look at these 'structures', as I have called them. These all represent peoples' different approaches to how the church should be run and the faith practised. I have my own opinions, but generally speaking, there are a range of views on each, and while I may express my views, it is important for me to acknowledge that other views, even contrary views, are also valid providing they are not contrary to Biblical guidance (and this is where it gets murky!).

Organisational Hierarchy:

> The extremes range from centralised governance of the church with one ultimate leader at the top (Catholicism, Anglicanism) to autonomous, self-governing local church bodies, usually committed to a set of principles and rules agreed upon by the denomination (Baptists, Assemblies of God). Corruption, intolerance and bureaucracy are the pitfalls of the former (centralised governance) with examples being the corrupt papacy of the middle ages, the intolerance of the Church of England leading to the emigration to America for religious freedom, and the difficulty these denominations face when dealing with current issues of female priests, homosexuality, and abortion legislation.

On the other hand, heresy and excess are the pitfalls of the latter (autonomous, self-governance) with examples being the ultra-conservative churches that have sprung up spouting hate and condemnation (Westboro Baptist Church in the USA) or the extreme charismatic churches that elevate personal prophecy above scripture and develop cult-like compliance and devotion to the organisation.

Most of the other Christian denominations fall somewhere between these two positions. The Presbyterian Church has a General Assembly while the Methodist Church has a 3-pronged General Conference, Council of Bishops, and Judicial Council. And the other denominations have various permutations of governance.

Baptism:

Baptism, considered by most (but not all) Christians to be a sacrament, was initiated by John the Baptist as a personal, and public, declaration of repentance from sin by symbolising the washing away of uncleanness through immersion in water. Jesus then made this a recognised step to be taken by all those who would follow Him, when he himself was baptised by John the Baptist after saying 'it is proper for us to do this to fulfil all righteousness'. Later He told His disciples to 'go and make disciples of all nations, baptising them in the name of the Father and of the Son and of the Holy Spirit'.

While all Christians support baptism, the issues of how and when became contentious. The how ranges from full immersion in water to sprinkling with water (usually on the head), and the when varies from birth to an age where a person could confess their belief (believers baptism). There is even a mention of baptism for the dead in 1 Corinthians. This (method and time of baptism) is the issue that originally distinguished the Baptist denomination (formerly Anabaptists), from other denominations, such as the Presbyterians. The Baptist denomination requires believer's baptism by full immersion, while the Presbyterians go with infant baptism by sprinkling. All the other denominations fall somewhere in this spectrum.

Spiritual Gifts:

In 1 Corinthians 12, the Apostle Paul gives a list of what is commonly recognised today as the Spiritual Gifts. Many denominations view these as apostolic gifts available to the apostles in the early church, but not generally available thereafter. Other denominations view these as gifts bestowed on Christians from Pentecost (the pouring out of the Holy Spirit on the Apostles in Acts 2) until today. The list of Spiritual Gifts is as follows: Wisdom, special knowledge, special faith, miraculous healing, other miraculous works, prophecy, special spiritual discernment, speaking in tongues and interpreting what is spoken in tongues. Examples of all of these can be seen by Jesus' followers in the book of Acts and the letters of Paul, in the New Testament.

The application and use of these Spiritual Gifts is foundational to the Pentecostal Movement that roughly started in 1906, and thus a common element of all 'Pentecostal' churches regardless of denomination. For instance, in the Baptist denomination you will see churches ranging from the very conservative (Spiritual Gifts do not apply today) to the fully Pentecostal (regular encouragement and exercising of the Spiritual Gifts), and the same applies to several other denominations, showing how the movement cuts across denominational boundaries.

Strangely, you would think that it is easily proven one way or the other as to whether the Spiritual

Gifts apply today, but in reality, what people are resolved to believe seems stronger than objective evidence. For example, Bethel Church in Redding California is known worldwide for its everyday experience across the full range of the Spiritual Gifts, while other churches, or denominations even, claim alternative explanations for the phenomena seen or simply choose to ignore it altogether. This issue, however, becomes very significant to the behaviour and practice of a church, hence it has become one of the most significant issues in choosing which church to attend or join.

Liturgy:

Liturgy, as I am referring to it, is the style, form, or even choreographed routine of the church service, as well as the formulated texts used throughout the service. It can vary widely between denominations, but it can also vary widely between churches within a denomination. The range can be from a completely prescribed service where every action (stand up, sit down, recite or read text, listen, kneel, sing, take communion, etc.) is the same from one week to the next, to the almost non-liturgical church service with no prescribed actions or texts, but a general pattern such as singing and sermon or maybe quiet meditation.

Worship:

> Worship, generally, is characterised by singing in most Christian churches, and nearly all church services, across nearly all denominations (except maybe the Quakers) have some form of worship / singing in their regular service. However, this singing can range from songs in pre-1900 hymnals, to updated hymnals, chorus books, more recent contemporary choruses, spontaneous singing or exclamation, or even chanting. It can be acappella or accompanied by organ, keyboard, guitar, or whole band and be with or without a church choir. And once again, this not only varies between denominations, but also between churches within a denomination.

Doctrinal Conservatism:

> The Christian faith is in Jesus Christ, our Saviour, as presented to us in the Bible. However, our Christian faith has both a doctrinal and an experiential element to it – sometimes referred to as a personal relationship with God / Jesus. As discussed previously, the Bible is the doctrinal basis for Christianity, but as Christians, we grow

increasingly aware of God's presence and influence in our lives: His comfort, His guidance, His inspiration, His providing, His forgiveness, His discipline, His love, His grace, His peace, His joy and His power. These are experienced subjectively, but none-the-less add to, or help to shape, our faith.

Doctrinal conservatism relates primarily to the interpretation of the Bible, but also to the degree of experiential influence tolerated. In terms of Biblical interpretation, the least conservative (or liberal) would believe the Bible has some divine inspiration, giving it spiritual reliability but not historical or factual reliability. It would view creation, the flood, tower of Babel, Moses crossing of the Red Sea, and just about all the miraculous stories in the Bible to be just stories, not factual, but conveying some spiritual significance. On the other end of the spectrum are the most conservative, or literalists, who claim every word of the Bible to be divinely inspired and hold to a very literal, or **their** literal, interpretation. This view would hold to the 6 days of creation being literal, 24 hour days (despite the sun not shining until day 4...), and they tend to try to apply a literal interpretation to the prophetic books, particularly

Revelation, which others would argue is allegorical, and not literal, to begin with.

So the various denominations tend to fall somewhere in this spectrum from liberal to conservative, and even ultra-conservative. Often, a single denomination may span quite a large range of the spectrum (eg. Anglican) with the churches of that denomination expressing their own specific place in the spectrum. Generally speaking, the Baptist and Southern Baptist denominations tend to be theologically conservative while the Presbyterian Church USA tends to be quite liberal (not to be confused with the Presbyterian Church In America which is conservative). Some, like the Plymouth Brethren, tend to be even more conservative than most Baptists, and the degree of conservatism of a denomination is usually reflected in the teaching at its Bible colleges or seminaries.

Chapter 4 Beware the Wolves: What to avoid?

There is no one perfect church to go to, nor is there a best church to recommend as, like it or not, we all have different tastes for the people and attitudes we want to grow in faith with. Some prefer more outward expression with uplifted hands, maybe dancing, maybe frequent prophetic utterances; while others may prefer less expression and more teaching; and others more contemplative and prayerful meetings; and still others more highly structured meetings with an Order of Service or Program of Service. What is important about the church we go to is:

- That it helps and encourages us to grow in our faith and trust in Jesus Christ our Saviour and Lord
- That we can build healthy and supportive relationships with others at that church
- That it equips and encourages us to engage more constructively with the world around us rather than withdraw or alienate ourselves from the world around us.

And I'm sure many would add to this list, and some may omit my third bullet point, but the point is to meet together in communal worship, teaching and prayer. However, in this section, my focus is not on what a church should include, but rather on what a church should avoid

– or what we should avoid in seeking a church to unite with.

Here is my **brief** list of what to avoid in a church (no doubt a much longer list could be formulated):

- Heavy shepherding
- Dogmatic scriptural interpretation
- Over emphasis on prophecy
- Over reliance on a formal liturgy
- The social gospel and Humanism
- Cults, communes and legalism

So let's tackle them in turn:

Heavy Shepherding

In some churches, the leaders of the church start instructing members of the church in what roles they should undertake in the church, in what practices or activities they should undertake outside of the church, in what financial contributions they should make to the church, in what their 'calling' from the Lord is, or even in where they should live or what employment they should have. This is called Heavy Shepherding. It is perfectly normal to seek advice from church leaders on any or all of these matters, but it is a step too far when the leaders try to instruct or dictate to members in any of these matters. They are manipulating and trying to use their 'spiritual maturity' or 'spiritual authority' over others to make them do their bidding, and this is not what Jesus taught us to do.

Dogmatic Scriptural Interpretation

As Christians, we believe that the Bible is God's written word to us. As previously discussed, the degree of inspiration of our modern English Bible translation, or even the King James version or the Latin Vulgate or even earlier manuscripts is debated among Christians, but we all still receive it as God's objective communication to mankind. However, how we receive and interpret the passages of the Bible will, at times, be subjective. Generally speaking, I, along with most Christians, almost subconsciously follow a simple guideline as follows:

1. What is the literal meaning of the words. This is usually the intended meaning for most passages that are not clearly allegorical.
2. Is the literal meaning consistent with the rest of the Bible – it should be.
3. Does the literal meaning have contextual or historical considerations regarding how we interpret or apply it now (or don't apply it)? This particularly applies to the Mosaic Law, some writings of Paul (eg. women's and men's hair,

women speaking in church, etc.), Daniel and the prophecy books, Revelation and more.
4. Is the interpretation and application of the passage consistent with the message of Jesus in the Gospels.
5. What is the Holy Spirit saying to me in this passage?

Yes, some people's interpretations of passages will be wrong, sometimes my interpretation will be wrong, although generally it is shades of grey rather than black and white, but the problem arises when some Christians, and some Christian teachers adopt a dogmatic approach that only their interpretation is right or valid. This sort of approach leads to churches like the Westboro Baptist Church in Kansas or other, typically ultra-right-wing dominated churches, where a particular leader insists that he or she has the pre-eminent understanding. They don't!

Over Emphasis (and under emphasis) of Prophecy

God loves us and God communicates with us, but do we 'hear' Him? There are occasions where God has communicated to people with an audible voice; the burning bush, the baptism of Jesus, the Transfiguration of Jesus, and more. There are people who claim to have heard an audible voice which they ascribe to God, and many of them I believe, but most of the time, when God speaks to us, it is as a quiet inspiration in our thoughts. This quiet inspiration (whether subconscious guidance, conscious thoughts, wisdom or understanding, words of knowledge (information we would have had no way of knowing)) is generally what we call the work of the Holy Spirit, and it is a very important element of our Christian faith and life. The word 'prophecy' as it is generally used in the church today refers primarily to Words of Knowledge and Information about the Future, as well as warnings about a possible future, and this is where a reasonable balance is needed.

Some churches reject the prospect of prophets today and God communicating to them with special messages to His church. These churches believe that further prophecy ended with the lifetimes of the '12' apostles and the sealing of the book of Revelation. Other churches believe that all Christians have access to the gift of prophecy and encourage the exercise of this gift on an ongoing basis. Some of these churches even thrive on a regular diet of prophecy, expecting and expressing prophecy in all their meetings, to the extent that they become obsessed with it (my opinion).

It is my opinion that both these extremes are to be avoided. The former because God should not, and is not, limited in His capacity and willingness to communicate to

His Church, and we, His Church, should never have our ears closed to Him. The Canon (Scripture) is sealed, but that does not preclude ongoing messages from God. And the latter is to be avoided because it leads to the over-reliance on prophecy (which can be highly subjective or even false) at the expense of reliance on the scriptures, which is a first step in deviation from the core Christian faith. This is often where cults or deviant doctrines get started.

Over Reliance on Routine Religious Practice

What I think of as the stereotypical church service would be the type where a program is handed out on the way in and every element of the service is prescribed; the sequence, the hymns, the prayers and declarations, when to stand and sit, and in some cases even the words spoken by the minister or priest. In current times, most services include some sort of sermon or epistle ranging from 5 to 30 minutes which is prepared in advance, but not prescribed as far as content or wording. In some more formal Church of England services, the Bible readings, prayers, and hymns are planned out months in advance (if not longer) and the communion (or mass) is shared in the same way every week. A lot of thought, and perhaps prayer, goes into the planning of these things, with every step and statement having significance, but how much thought or prayer goes into the **practice** of every step and statement by the members of the congregation?

For myself, I have found that the first time through such a church service, I value, and feel aware of, the significance of the actions and recitations, but by about the third time, I find myself reciting, standing, sitting and singing on autopilot with little appreciation of the significance whatsoever. When this takes place week after week, it becomes a religious practice with the only element really touching my consciousness being the sermon, and this is the problem – religious practice. What, if any, is the benefit of religious practice? And how subtly and easily does our faith in Jesus slip into a faith in religious practice? If there was one statement that would ban a person from heaven, it would be, 'I have been a good, practising Christian.' The access to heaven, to eternal life with God, is on the basis of Jesus' atonement for our sins and not our religious practice.

Repetitive, highly structured, religious practice in church services does not work for me, but I can accept that it may work for some, enabling them to better encounter God's presence or to more sincerely express their worship to God. However, we all must be wary of falling into reliance on religious practice, and hence I list this as something to avoid in choosing a church.

The Rational Choice

The Social Gospel and Humanism

Back in the 1990s, I attended a day hosted by Christian Aid involving a few workshops and talks. In the entire day, I could not recall the word, 'God', being mentioned once, much less the name, Jesus, or the Holy Spirit. The workshops looked at typical scenarios of need, usually 3rd world, such as drought or refugee camps, and asked the participants to brainstorm ideas of what could or should be done. It was useful, informative, much needed and good, and my aim here is not to criticise it, but the speakers and workshop leaders completely omitted or disregarded any notion of God or prayer being any part of a solution. Christian Aid, on that day, with those particular leaders, was being presented as a secular organisation, not a Christian one. (I do not mean this about Christian Aid generally.) Their motives were good, out of their love and concern for our fellow humanity, and their efforts and sacrifices are to be commended, and supported, but on that day, it did not come across as rooted in Christian faith. So what? What is my point?

As Jesus is quoted as saying in the gospels, "Love the Lord your God with all your heart and with all your soul and with all your mind. This is the first and greatest commandment. And the second is like it, Love your neighbour as yourself." Omitting the first, and greatest commandment is not Christian, and it is omitting the very purpose of our existence, to enter into a loving and eternal relationship with God...and our fellow humanity. The love of God is foundational, with the love of our neighbour built upon it. Humanism, or its twin in the guise of Christianity (the Social Gospel), tries to echo the 'love your neighbour' principle, but it can find no source of value in people apart from a shared identity. The Christian values and loves his/her neighbour because God does, and therefore their neighbour is worthy of their love – even if they're not very likeable. Corrie Ten Boom, a Holocaust survivor, could forgive and value a cruel guard from the concentration camp she was in because she knew that God valued and loved the man, despite his horrific past.

However, my purpose here is to highlight what to avoid in a Christian church, and this Social Gospel or Humanism can be a very subtle and deceptive diversion leading away from Christian faith. All churches have a certain focus on helping others in need, whether in their community or further afield, and so we are all encouraged to engage with these good works – and that is right and good. But the church where this is the sole or primary focus, above the love and pursuit of God, is to be avoided because it will eventually choke out the love and pursuit of God that was beginning to germinate.

The Rational Choice

Cults, Communes and Legalism

This last area to avoid is a bit of a catch-all. Any church or body of people, claiming to be Christian but having a unique practice that sets them apart from the rest of the Christian community is to be eyed warily. The Children of God cult (now known as The Family International or TFI) is an example of such a church. They claim faith in Jesus Christ as their Saviour and Lord, and they study their Bibles and preach in public to win others to the faith (or is it to their church), but their focus on an imminent Apocalypse, was started by the teaching of one man (David Berg). They reject the established Christian churches as ineffective and lacking understanding or revelation, they live in communities or communes, and they use sexual promiscuity to recruit new members. One of their most notable doctrines has been that sex was an expression of the love of God and that it should not be limited by age or relationship, which of course resulted in child sexual abuse, manipulative rape, etc.. They exercise physical discipline of members, require members to bring in finance and train members in lying to and manipulating "outsiders".

Legalism, or the **requirement** to act in a certain manner or adhere to a particular practice or follow a specific rule in order to be an acceptable or "good" Christian is common among cults, but it also weaves its tentacles into mainstream churches. The pressure to be a 'good' Christian comes from within the church as well as from outside the church (eg. "You say you are a Christian, so why didn't you..."). Yes, we want to be good ambassadors for the Christian faith and we want to live lives pleasing to God, but God has bestowed upon us His Holy Spirit to work in us and change us to become faithful followers of Jesus, along with the Bible to transform our thinking. Our work is to listen to and be led by His Holy Spirit, not to listen to and be led by the rules that others try to impose upon us; and we are to read the Bible and allow it to transform our minds. Beware of churches that try to impose their rules or expectations on the people of their congregations. And certainly, your salvation depends on your belief in Jesus as your Saviour and Lord, not on how 'good' a Christian you have been or on how well you follow the rules or expectations of a church.

Jesus surrendered his life to the Jews and the Gentiles (the Romans) as a sacrifice to redeem each one of us (Jews or Gentiles) so that we could be children of God. His sacrifice earned us salvation, not any of our achievements, and certainly not any obedience to some prescribed church rules.

Chapter 5 Find a Church

In Summary

Finally, find a church that helps you grow in your faith in Jesus Christ, in your knowledge, understanding, and love of God, and in your love of and service to all mankind. Watch out for and avoid the things I have mentioned but remember that no Earthly church is perfect, just as not one of us is perfect, so be patient, kind and forgiving. Without a local church you are vulnerable to;

- the weeds of this world choking out your faith,
- the lies of this world or the lies of our own fleshly hearts corrupting our faith,
- or our love towards our brothers and sisters in Christ being stifled for lack of opportunity for expression and growth.

Make church attendance and involvement a habit, but not a legalistic duty, and look upon it as a privilege and a kindness from God. The Church, in scripture, is referred to as the Bride of Christ being made ready for His return. We, the believers in these local churches, are all a part of Christ's Bride, so we are to cherish one another as Christ cherishes each one of us.

The Rational Choice

Acknowledgments

I wish to thank all of those who contributed to my faith and the writing and publishing of this book:

Vicki McGlashen – whose prayers for me nearly 50 years ago were answered.

Pavel and Clara Steiger – who led me to the Lord nearly 40 years ago.

Dave Roberts – who prophesied that the Lord had placed a book in me, to be written.

Tony Balio – whose feedback and edit were of great value to me.

Beccy Morton - whose encouragement in the publishing process helped push me over the line.

My children - for prodding me to complete this.

And to the countless many for their encouragement along the way.

About the Author

I am a Christian, and a Physics teacher living in Surrey, UK. My Christian faith started back in 1986, while working for an oil company in Indonesia, through the rational dismantling of my evolutionary mindset born out of my American education. My prayer, back in 1967 at the age of 11, for God to show me the proof that He exists, was answered. Sharing that proof, or rational evidence, became the driving force behind the writing of this book, so that my own children, as well as all other readers of this book, can be enabled to make a rational choice to know God.

My life as a Christian has had its ups and downs with much refining of my character, my understanding, and my perspective on the Church. The second half of this book reflects my concern for Christians, particularly new Christians, navigating the complex and challenging edifice of our Church.

Printed in Great Britain
by Amazon